The
Illuminati Papers

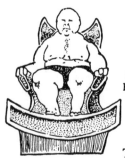

Bavarian Illuminati

Founded by Hassan i Sabbah, 1090 A.D. (5090 A.L., 4850 A.M.)
Reformed by Adam Weishaupt, 1776 A.D. (5776 A.L., 5536 A.M.)

THE ANCIENT ILLUMINATED SEERS OF BAVARIA

invite YOU to join

The World's Oldest and Most Successful Conspiracy

Don't Let THEM
Immanentize th
Eschaton

Have you ever SECRETLY WONDERED WHY the GREAT PYRAMID has FIVE sides (counting the bottom)?

WHAT IS the TRUE secret SINISTER REALITY lying behind the ANCIENT Aztec Legend of QUETZALCOATL?

WHO IS the MAN in ZURICH that some SWEAR is **LEE HARVEY OSWALD**?

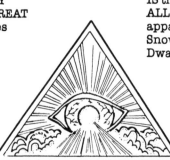

IS there an ESOTERIC ALLEGORY concealed in the apparently innocent legend of Snow White and the Seven Dwarfs?

WHY do scholarly anthropologists TURN PALE with terror at the very MENTION of the FORBIDDEN name YOG-SOTHOTH?

WHAT REALLY DID HAPPEN TO AMBROSE BIERCE?

If your I.Q. is over 150, and you have $3,125.00 (plus handling), you **might** be eligible for a trial membership in the A.I.S.B. If you think you qualify, put the money in a cigar box and bury it in your backyard. One of our Underground Agents will contact you shortly.

I DARE YOU!

TELL NO ONE: ACCIDENTS HAVE A STRANGE WAY OF HAPPENING TO PEOPLE WHO TALK TOO MUCH ABOUT THE BAVARIAN ILLUMINATI!

May we warn you against imitations!
Ours is the original and genuine

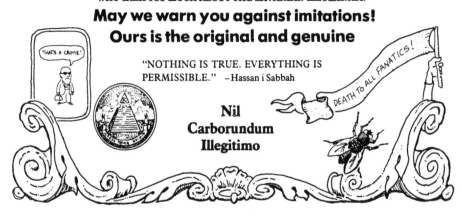

"NOTHING IS TRUE. EVERYTHING IS PERMISSIBLE." – Hassan i Sabbah

THAT'S A CRIME!

DEATH TO ALL FANATICS!

Nil
Carborundum
Illegitimo

The Illuminati Papers

Robert Anton Wilson

Ronin Publishing, Inc.

The Illuminati Papers
ISBN: 0-157951-002-7
ISBN: 978-1-57951-002-2
Copyright © 1980, 1997 by Robert Anton Wilson

Published by **RONIN Publishing, Inc.**
PO Box 22900
Oakland, CA 94609
www.roninpub.com

Project Editor:	Sebastian Orfali
Cover Design:	Judy July, Generic Type
Cover Production:	Rick Greer, Generic Type
Cover Drawing:	Jon Thompson from *Cosmic Trigger*
	© 1976 by Robert Anton Wilson

Originally published by And/Or Press, Inc.

Printed in the USA

Library of Congress Cataloging in Publication Data
Wilson, Robert Anton, 1932 - 2002
    The Illuminati Papers

        1. Occult science - Miscellanea   I. Title
BF1999.W626   009.9   80-16641

Imprimatur
Mordecai the Foul, High priest,
Head temple, Bavarian Illuminati

Nihil Obstat
Theophobia the Elder, House of
Apostles of Eris, Discordian Society

Non Illegitimati
Carborundum
Frater Soror, Elect of Nine, Council
of Ordinals, Collegium Rosa Crucis

Class "A" Publication
Ancient Illuminated Seers of
Bavaria

Ewige Blumenkraft
This is an important historical
document. Do not use these pages as
toilet tissue.

Contents

Glossary 1
ITEM   Join the HEAD Revolution 3
The Abolition of Stupidity 4
    by Hagbard Celine
Neophobia/Neophilia Quiz 10
ITEM   A Few of the Things
    I Know About Her 13
    by Simon Moon
Quantum Mechanics as a Branch
of Primate Psychology 15
    by Simon Moon
Dissociation of Ideas, 1 17
ITEM   The Eight Circuits
    of the Nervous System 17
Conspiracy Digest, Interview 1 19
Neuroeconomics 25
    by Hagbard Celine
Dissociation of Ideas, 2 31
Coex! Coex! Coex! 31
From: The Order of the Illuminati,
    Sirius Section 35
To: Galactic Central
ITEM   Hey, man, are you using
    only half your brain? 39
Conspiracy Digest, Interview 2 40
Science Fiction Review, Interview 1 46
ITEM   Top Secret 48
Ten Good Reasons to Get Out of Bed
in the Morning 50
Dissociation of Ideas, 3 58
ITEM   Daddy, Why Did God
    Make Us? 59
ITEM   60
Beethoven as Information 62
    by Justin Case

ITEM   Addendum 65
Science Fiction Review, Interview 2 66
Mammalian Politics:
Thackeray Via Kubrick 68
    by Justin Case
ITEM   The Eight Basic
    Winner Scripts 71
An Incident on Cumberland Avenue 72
ITEM   Sir, are you using
    only half your brain? 83
Conspiracy Digest, Interview 3 84
ITEM   92
ITEM   The Eight Basic
    Loser Scripts 93
Beyond Theology:
The Science of Godmanship 94
The Goddess of Ezra Pound 103
    by Mary Margaret Wildeblood
Conspiracy Digest, Interview 4 109
ITEM   Bavarian Illuminati 112
    This is a Magick Letter
Conspiracy Digest, Interview 5 114
Dissociation of Ideas, 4 117
ITEM   Lawrence Talbot Suite 117
    by Simon Moon
Celine's Laws 118
    by Hagbard Celine
Infinite Cruelty 126
    by Epicene Wildeblood
ITEM   Riddle Song 132
    by Robin Marian
Stupidynamics 132
    by Simon Moon
Paleopuritanism and Neopuritanism 138
    by Marvin Gardens
ITEM   Art Is Technology:
    Technology Is Art 143
ITEM   Nine Million Dead 144
    by Simon Moon
The RICH Economy 145
    by Mordecai the Foul, High Priest,
    Head Temple, Bavarian Illuminati
Dissociation of Ideas, 5 149

"I contradict myself?
Very well, then: I contradict myself.
I am large: I contain multitudes."

Walt Whitman

"The opposite of a trivial truth is false;
the opposite of a great truth is also true."

Niels Bohr

"Time is three eyes and eight elbows."

Dogen Zenji

"I'll pick-a you up in my car."
"Oh, you have a car?"
"No. I used to have a car and a chauffeur, but
I couldn't afford both, so I got rid of the car."
"What good is a chauffeur without a car?"
"I need him to drive me to work."
"How can he drive you to work without a car?"
"It's-a okay. I don't have a job."

Chico and Groucho, *Duck Soup*

Introduction

Future events like these will
effect you in the future!
—*Plan 9 From Outer Space*

Does zoology include humans?
—*Marnie*

This book dates from a barbaric, almost pre-historic age—over twenty years ago. You will realize how far back in the abyss of time that near-Feudal epoch looks in retrospect when I tell you that I wrote the entire manuscript on a *typewriter*. Of course, we had electric lights instead of candles, and the "horseless carriage" had come into general use, but otherwise the so-called advanced nations remained in a primitive industrial economy and few could foresee the Information Age dawning.

Those Eolithic days seem hard to recall now. Nobody but the military and a few universities had access to Internet or the World Wide Web; if I wanted to do research, I had to leave the *"typewriter"* — a device only a little less archaic than the quill pen—and drive to a library where I'd spend a day *taking notes with a pen on a pad*. No humans lived in space

yet; the Mir space station did not begin construction until 1986, eight years after *The Illuminati Papers* appeared. Most of what I wrote then seemed as fabulous as Oz or Wonderland to the majority of readers; now, I fear some readers will find parts of this hackneyed—except in the Manhattan Literary Establishment, where these ideas are still considered wild and crazy. (Those New Yorkers still seem to think the latest radical notions are those of Freud and Marx.)

Even the first long (or longish) chapter in this book, "The Abolition of Stupidity," dealing with intelligence-raising technologies, seemed like fantasy or satire to most 1970s readers. By comparison, if you hunt around the World Wide Web today, you will find over 1000 entries, dealing with DHEA, "Blast," Hydergine and dozens of other brain-boosting substances. Since I can safely assume most of my readers have Web access by now, let me suggest that you find out how this field has developed by clicking on *smart drugs* in the Extropian web site at

http://www.c2org/~arkuat/extr/.

Back in the '70s, most critics did not know what the hell to make out of these pages and generally classified the whole book as science fiction in disguise. Fortunately, readers as a group do not have the rear-view vision that seems required of posh reviewers, and many of them understood me very well. Every year now, and in fact many times a year, I meet people who tell me their choice of career resulted from reading my science faction. (Most of these people went into space engineering, psychopharmacology, life extension research or quantum physics.)

Looking back, I feel a sense of humble astonishment. I seem to have written a 1990s book in the 1970s. Only in the matter of computer networking do I appear to have missed the boat: I knew major changes would come, but I did not know enough about that field to know how rapidly or how totally the cyber-revolution would shake, quake and remake our society. Otherwise, my forecasts of the coming waves of change in space migration, longevity, and automation seem good enough to tempt me to set up shop as a fortune teller. But I did not use any "psychic" powers in my future-scans; I used simple common-sense projections of trends that had become more and more obvious throughout human history.

• **Space Migration:** Whenever new territory becomes habitable, humans move in, so it did not require shamanic talent to foresee a migration into space.

• **Life Extension:** Ever since science escaped from the tyranny of the Romish Inquisition, life span has steadily increased, from less than 40 years in the 18th Century, to 50 years at the end of the 19th, to 60 years around 1950, to 73+ for males and 78+ for females in the advanced nations today. With the research on gerontology already underway when I wrote this book, it required no genius to foresee the Life Extension Revolution, in which millions of people now use compounds with a high probability of increasing life span ever further, and thousands of researchers optimistically look forward to breakthroughs that will give us lives that measure centuries rather than decades.

• **Intelligence Increase:** My crystal ball, however, seems to have been cloudy on the subject of Intelligence Increase. Despite all the people using the "smart drugs" mentioned above, the majority, at least in the U.S., has grown steadily stupider. I attribute this to a deliberate policy of "dumbing down" the population, instigated by our ruling Elite after the donnybrooks and *katzenjammerei* of the '60s taught them that too many educated people represented a real danger to the *status quo*. Arlen, my wife, often claims that nobody educated since 1975 seems to know *anything*, and Kurt Vonnegut has made the same observation. I don't think the situation has gotten quite that bad really: only the majority of Generation X seems to think Einstein invented the telescope or that the Bill of Rights says the government has the right to screw us any way it wants; a saving minority, even among the under-30, seems as bright as the best minds of *any* generation.

A few sections of this book discuss our nation's rapid movement toward totalitarianism (perhaps too satirically for such a grim subject; some people thought I was joking...) These passages now seem, strangely, rather understated. In this connection, let me cite a recent article by Claire Wolfe[1] which rather clearly shows that our present urine testing by the Piss Police only represents a small part of the Kafkaization of this once-free Republic. Wolfe lists some of the fascist laws enacted by the 104th Congress:

• A law establishing a national database of employed people. After this is implemented, only the homeless, the hermits and the subterraneans will remain free of federal snooping.
• 100 pages of new laws creating scores of new "health care" crimes for departures from A.M.A. dogma. The penalties for such heresy include, but are not limited to, seizure of assets from both doctors and patients.
• Laws allowing confiscation of assets from any escapee who establishes foreign citizenship. (If you run, like the Jews who got out of Nazi Germany, reconcile yourself to leaving everything valuable behind.)
• The largest gun confiscation act in U.S. history.
• Increased funding for the already Gestapo-like Bureau of Alcohol, Tobacco, and Firearms, the people responsible for perpetrating the Waco holocaust. (By the way, have you checked

[1] "Land-Mine Legislation," by Claire Wolfe, 1997 Summer Supplement, Loompanics Unlimited, Port Towsend WA.

to find out if *your* church is BATF approved?)
• A law enabling the government to declare any group "terrorist" by fiat, *without trial and without appeal.* Such groups will then have to turn membership lists over to the Feds.
• Laws allowing secret trials with secret evidence for various classes of defendants.
• A law requiring States to begin issuing driver's licenses only with security features (such as fingerprints, social security numbers etc.) by October 1st, 2000. You won't be able to drive without giving the Feds all the data they need to snoop into all your private affairs; if that much surveillance makes you nervous, learn to hoof it.
• A law establishing a national database containing everything your doctor and you say during consultation. If you don't like the Feds knowing all about your recent bout of the clap, or even about your vaginal yeast infection, you might think of running for the border right away; see the third item above, about forfeiture laws.

If you think this is some of kind of joke or satire that Wolfe or I invented, look up the article I'm citing. Wolfe gives the names and numbers of all these laws. For instance, the last one listed, mandating invasion of the privacy of the doctor's office, appears in sections 262-264 of HR 3103, the innocently titled Health Insurance Portability and Accountability Act of 1996. Wolfe calls these statutes "land mines" because they are all hidden in bills with similarly innocuous titles.

The amusing thing (if you can still feel amused after reading the above) is that all this legislation was passed by a

Republican-dominated Congress, which got elected on a platform promising to "get the government off our backs." (Wilson's Fourth Law: Whatever politicians promise before election, they'll very probably do the opposite after election.) Even funnier, the Republicans still claim that so-called "liberal Democrats" represent the major threat to our liberties.

By the way, has anybody actually seen, heard, touched, or smelled a truly "liberal" democrat in the last 30 years? Or are there any rumors, yarns, or folklore about the survival of that seemingly extinct species emanating from anyone else but the Republicans?

Of course, even before the 104th Congress, you already had to give a urine sample whenever the Piss Police came along, and if any narc liked your country estate, he only had to plant a small amount of cocaine in the pantry to seize the building (and the grounds) from you *without a trial*. If the deliberate dumbing down of America hadn't been so successful, the majority of the population would be in open revolt by now; but a nation of sheep submits to the shears, and to the abattoir, without even bleating in alarm.

Indeed, Claire Wolfe, whose summary of recent fascist legislation I have paraphrased, comments wanly:

It is very risky to actively resist unbridled power...
For that reason, among many others, I would never recommend any particular course of action to anyone—and I hope you'll think twice before taking "advice" from anybody about things that could jeopardize your life or well-being.

Wolfe does mention, without endorsing, some of the methods that various brave souls have employed in the attempt to recapture some of our lost liberties—tax refusal; civil disobedience; non-cooperation with the authorities; boycotts; secession efforts; monkey-wrenching; computer hacking; dirty tricks; public shunning of government agents; alternative communities that provide their own medical care and utilities.

Whenever any of these tactics gets enough publicity or causes enough nuisance, the authorities react the way authorities can be expected to react. Never Forget Waco. Never.

Tax refusal, whatever brilliant legal arguments some libertarians produce to justify it, usually provokes confiscation of everything you own, and a jail term usually follows. Civil disobedience and non-cooperation can also land you in the can, or can escalate to Ruby Ridge massacres. Boycotts remain safe, if you can figure out the tactics carefully and have a lot of associates. Monkey-wrenching, computer hacking and dirty tricks remain popular, but also lead to jail if you get caught. Public shunning is both possible and legal; it happens increasingly in places like Idaho, Utah, Montana and Nevada. Alternative drop-out communities are only safe as long as they remain very low profile.

Now maybe you can see why I have so much enthusiasm for civilian space colonization.

That will still take quite a while. Meanwhile, you might consider migrating to *crypto-space*.

"Crypto-space" is my name for the part of cyberspace presently invisible to government snooping. As T.C. May writes:

Strong cryptography, exemplified by RSA (a public key algorithm) and PGP (Pretty Good Privacy) provides encryption that essentially cannot be broken with all the computing power in the universe...

Digital mixes, or anonymous remailers, use crypto to create untraceable e-mail...

Digital cash, untraceable and anonymous (like real cash) is also coming...[2]

J. Orlin Grabbe comments:

The government doesn't want you using cryptography because they want to know where you money is so they can get some of it. And they don't like you using drugs, unless the government is the dealer.[3]

In fact, virtual communities with virtual cash already exist in crypto-space. According to the *Encyclopedia of Social Inventions*,[4] the first non-interest bearing non-taxable virtual money came into existence in Vancouver in 1983. The idea has not received much publicity, but it spread as far south as San Diego by 1990.

Unlike Fed notes, virtual money—a form of barter—does not require interest, because virtual cash is created by the people who use it for their own convenience. Fed notes, on the other hand, are created precisely to bear interest, at as high a rate as the market will bear. Your share of the national debt is money you owe to the Fed for using their notes, which you have to use until you find the Doorway to Freedom and creep off into crypto-space. And virtual cash is tax-free because the IRS can't find it.

Evolution proceeds, it seems to me, by challenges which force organisms to get smarter. In a fascist state like Bill Clinton's U.S.A., the smartest will find ways out of the cage much more effective than the tactics of Randy Weaver on his mountain or the Republic of Texas, or similar groups still seeking freedom within geospace. *There is no freedom in geospace. Every square inch has been mapped and claimed by some nation or corporation or syndicate. The only remaining frontier is electronic.*

The Internet not only opens the door to freedom just when the Feds seem to have us locked up forever, but it also seems to make "desovereignization," as Buckminster Fuller called it, inevitable. According to Fuller's analysis, the Great Pirates—kings, emperors, mikadoes, prime ministers—who seized control of Terra at the beginning of the Bronze Age are now sponsored entities, puppets of finance capitalism. When Fuller wrote *Grunch of Giants*, it required $100,000,000 to run a campaign for president; it requires even more now, due to inflation. Guess where the politicians of the world get that kind of money, and then you'll have a good idea who really runs the world today.

Whether the Republicans or Democrats win an election, the Federal Reserve still makes the important decisions; whether the Tories or Labour win in England, the Bank of England remains

---

[2] "Crypto Anarchy and Virtual Communities," tcmay@netcom.com
[3] Grabbe, via tcmay above
[4] *Encyclopedia of Social Inventions*, Institute of Social Inventions, London, 1990.

in control. As Fuller wrote:

> Never before in all history have the
> inequities and the momentums of
> unthinking money-power been so
> glaringly evident to so vastly large a
> number of...all-around-the-world
> humans...[5]

For more details of how Fuller expects
these informed humans to "desover-
eignize" the planet, cooperatively "advan-
taging all without disadvantaging any"
through electronic speed-of-light synergy
with Internet, see

http://www.teleport.com/~pdx4d/grunch/html.

As I point out in "Celine's Laws,"
later in this volume, authoritarian communication is always blocked by
SNAFU; nobody tells the whole truth
about anything to those who have the
power to jail and kill. Libertarian communication, via Internet, allows for
quicker feedback, which will also be
more accurate feedback, and Spaceship
Earth will begin to move in a sensible
way at last, no longer having 150+
Supreme Commanders all steering in
different directions.

Until that planetary synergy (called
the Global Brain by British philosopher
Peter Russell) emerges fully, we still have
jury nullification, guaranteed *de jure* since
the Magna Carta and *de facto* unalien-
able. When you sit on a jury, no power on
earth can force you to find somebody
guilty in a case where you believe the law

itself is unconstitutional, tyrannous or
dangerous to your own civil liberties.
Here are a few citations which State
Education and the mass media try their
damnedest to keep you from ever seeing:

> Every jury in the land is tampered
> with and falsely instructed
> by the judge when it is told that it
> must accept as the law
> that which has been given to them,
> or that they can decide
> only the facts of the case.
>
> —Lord Denham[6]

> The jury has the power to bring in a
> verdict in the teeth of
> both the law and the facts.
>
> —Justice Oliver Wendell Holmes[7]

> If the jury feels the law is unjust, we
> recognize the undisputed
> power of the jury to acquit, even if
> its verdict is contrary to the
> law as given by a judge, and
> contrary to the evidence.
>
> —4th Circuit Court of Appeals[8]

> When a jury acquits a defendant
> even though he or she clearly
> appears to be guilty, the acquittal
> conveys significant information
> about community attitudes and
> provides a guideline for future
> prosecutorial discretion...Because
> of the high acquittal rate in
> prohibition cases in the 1920s and
> early 1930s, prohibition laws could
> not be enforced. The repeal of these

[5] *Grunch of Giants*, by R. Buckminster Fuller,
St. Martin's Press, NY, 1983, p 89.

[6] O'Connell v Rex, 1884.
[7] Horning v District of Columbia, 138 (1920).
[8] US v Moylan, 1969.

laws is traceable to the refusal of juries to convict those accused of alcohol traffic.

—Sheflin and Van Dyke [9]

For more details on how juries can protect our civil liberties even when the government is hell-bent on destroying them, see

http://nowscape.com/fija/fija_us.html.

The Chinese allegedly have a curse which says, "May you live in interesting times." We undoubtedly live in interesting times, but I don't find it a curse. As Nietzsche should have said, anything that doesn't kill me makes me smarter. The

evils of the world, which involve massive starvation as well as the erosion of individual liberty I have been discussing, challenge us to use our heads better, and the H.E.A.D. Revolution is what this book is all about.

Turn the page and you'll find even more reason to feel braced and excited about the problems we confront and our ability to deal with them. Solving problems is one of the highest and most sensual of all our brain functions.

Robert Anton Wilson
Freedom, California
23 May 1997

[9] *Law and Contemporary Problems*, 43, No 4, 1980.

Glossary

Consciousness
Information received and decoded by a structure. In prescientific human beings, the structure is the nervous system as defined and limited by its imprints.

Intelligence
Information received, decoded, and transmitted by a structure. Operationally, we cannot say an entity is "intelligent" until it transmits information received.

Imprints
Electrochemically bonded neural circuits defining and limiting the capacity to receive, decode, and transmit information. There are at least eight imprint circuits in the human, of which only four are normally used.

Higher consciousness
Neurological states in which suspension of imprint or serial reimprinting allow for detection of information usually not received by the four primitive circuits.

Higher intelligence
(1) Neurological training which allows for high-fidelity reception, decoding, and transmission on all eight circuits of the human nervous system. (2) Presumed extraterrestrial races which have evolved to such hi-fi information processing.

"Reality"
The Gestalts which a given nervous system integrates out of information received. Each "reality" is relative, being defined and limited by the imprint circuits of the receiving nervous system.

Brainwashing
Forcible reimprinting of a nervous system to eliminate old "realities" and imprint a new "reality."

Hedonic engineering
The art and science of reimprinting one's own nervous system for more ecstatic or intelligent functioning. Serial reincarnation in one body.

Information
The measure of the amount of order in a system. The mathematical reciprocal of *entropy*, the amount of *dis*order in a system.

Signal
A unit of information at a velocity equal to, or less than, the speed of light.

Electromagnetic chauvinism
The belief that information requires transportation, i.e., signals, i.e., energy moving at, or less than, the speed of light.

Neurologic
The logic of the nervous system; how the imprint circuits process information.

Terrestrial circuits
The imprint circuits concerned with survival, status, and reproduction in a gravity well, i.e., on the surface of a planet. These are the four circuits normally used by most human beings.

Left hemisphere
The portion of the brain concerned with linear processes. The presumed control center of the four terrestrial circuits.

Extraterrestrial circuits
The imprint circuits concerned with what have been called "religious" or "mystical" consciousness. These are now assumed to be the four circuits of quantum logic for use in space migration, higher intelligence, and longevity-immortality.

1

Right hemisphere
The presumed brain location of the quantum-logic circuits of extraterrestrial consciousness.

Light cone
An hour-glass-shaped figure in which the spacetime paths of light make up the cone itself. All *signals* move at, or slower than, the speed of light and must be *inside* the light cone. Thus, only events in the past light cone can affect *A*. And, in turn, *A* can affect only those events in its future light cone. This is the rule of special relativity. However, there may be quantum events that do have effects *outside* the light cone. These effects would have to be nonenergetic effects: information without transportation, or without signals.

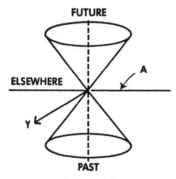

FUTURE

ELSEWHERE

A

Y

PAST

ERP
The Einstein-Rosen-Podolsky paradox, which holds that if quantum theory is true, *nonlocal* effects must occur (outside the light cone). This was offered as a *reductio ad absurdum* of quantum theory, since it suggests "telepathy," as Einstein pointed out.

Bell's theorem
John S. Bell's proof (1964) that any objective quantum theory must include nonlocal effects: effects outside the light cone (faster than light). Thus, if we reject nonlocality with its suggestion of "telepathy," we seem

driven to nonobjectivity, which suggests psychokinesis or the merging of physics and parapsychology into paraphysics.

Decoding
Finding the meaningful structure (information) within a system. Beethoven's *Ninth* and the Crick-Watson DNA model are both decodings of the life script of Terra.

Neuro-
A prefix denoting "known by or through the human nervous system." Thus we have no physics but neurophysics, no psychology but neuropsychology, no linguistics but neurolinguistics, and, ultimately, no neurology but neuroneurology, and no neuroneurology but neuroneuroneurology, etc. See *Von Neumann's catastrophe* immediately below.

Von Neumann's catastrophe
More fully known as Von Neumann's catastrophe of the infinite regress. A mathematical demonstration by John Von Neumann, showing that any attempt to remove uncertainty from the quantum realm by introducing a second order of instruments to monitor the first order will still contain uncertainty, leading to a third order of instruments, a fourth, etc., to infinity... or to a decision by the observer that we can bear the remaining amount of uncertainty.

Guerilla ontology
The basic technique of all my books. Ontology is the study of being; the guerilla approach is to so mix the elements of each book that the reader must decide on each page "How much of this is real and how much is a put-on?" This literary technique seems justified by the accelerated acceleration of new knowledge, new theories, new inventions, and new possibilities in our time, since any "reality" map we can form is probably obsolete by the time it reaches print.

𝔍tem

Join the HEAD Revolution

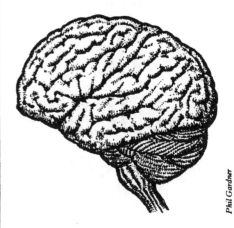

Want to contact Higher Intelligence? It's easy, really.

The human brain is an "organ of adaptation" (Freud).

HEAD means *Hedonic Engineering and Development.*

Using your brain for fun and profit. Efficiently, ecstatically, creatively. Contacting the Higher Intelligence *within.*

That's what HEAD is all about. Having fun with your own HEAD. And getting smarter.

Send us no money. Just buy the basic programming manuals for the human HEAD:

1. The book you have in your hands.

2. *Exo-Psychology,* by Timothy Leary, Ph.D.

3. *Programming and Metaprogramming in the Human Biocomputer,* by John Lilly, M.D.

Phil Gardner

4. *Mind Games,* by Masters and Houston.

5. *Magick,* by Aleister Crowley.

That's all there is to it. Read the manuals. Learn to program your own HEAD space. Be the first Hedonic Engineer on your block.

And . . . have fun with your new Head!

Illuminati International

LEIF ERIKSON CABAL, LEGION OF DYNAMIC DISCORD, POSITION PAPER #00001

The Abolition of Stupidity

by Hagbard Celine

Two eminently intelligent men, R. Buckminster Fuller and Werner Erhard, have proposed that we can and should abolish starvation by the end of this century.

This goal is rational, practical, and desirable; so it is naturally denounced as Utopian, fantastic, and absurd.

I wish to propose a similar goal, which is also rational, practical, and desirable, and which will also be denounced as Utopian, fantastic, and absurd.

I suggest a worldwide War against Stupidity.

Although the stupid will naturally resent this, I address my ideas here to those who are not totally stupid or who are not stupid all the time, i.e., those rare individuals who have occasional lucid moments.

The arguments for this Revolutionary Notion are as follows:

1. Although one sounds like a satirist to say it, this planet does seem to be controlled by and largely populated by persons who are not in all respects reasonable men and women. Voltaire, of course, may have been exaggerating when he said that the only way to understand the mathematical concept of infinity is to contemplate the extent of human stupidity; but the situation is almost that bad. To mention just a few examples from my own lifetime: Hitler murdered six million Jews for "reasons" that were totally insane; Senator Joe McCarthy led a crazy witch-hunt against Communists which ruined many innocent people and never succeeded in uncovering one absolutely definitive real Communist; Anita Bryant is currently waging a crusade right out of the thirteenth century against homosexuals; etc.

It is scarcely an exaggeration to say that millions of humans have been murdered in the course of such irrational scapegoating throughout history. Since each of us belongs to some minority or other, any of us might be one of the targets in the next witch-hunt, and if they burn us there will be nothing left to cryonically preserve.

Nor is stupidity the exclusive trait of the stupid; you do not need a "vocation" for it, as you do for the priesthood. It seems to be a contagious socio-semantic disturbance which afflicts all of us at one time or another. Notorious examples can be found in the lives of "the Great," such as Simon Newcombe (the astronomer who discovered Neptune) "proving" mathematically that heavier-than-air flight was impossible, the French Academy refusing to examine the evidence for meteorites in the eighteenth century, etc. (Some might include Einstein's continuous attempts to refute the random factor in quantum mechanics as

4

another example of stupidity in a fine mind.)

More generally, as Thomas Kuhn has shown in *The Structure of Scientific Revolutions*, an exact measurement of the extent of stupidity among the learned is provided by the fact that every scientific revolution seems to take a generation. As Kuhn documents extensively, this one-generation time-lag seems to be caused by the fact that elderly scientists hardly ever accept a new model, however good it is, and the revolution is only fully accomplished when a second generation, with less prejudice, examines both the new and old models objectively and determines that the new is more useful.

But if science, the paradigm of rationality, is infested with enough stupidity to cause this generalized one-generation lag, what can we say of politics, economics, and religion? Time-lags of thousands of years seem to be normal in those areas.

Indeed, it was chiefly by contemplating religious history that Voltaire was led to conclude that human stupidity approximated to the infinite. The study of politics is hardly more inspiring, and any examination of economic debate strongly suggests that the theologians of the Dark Ages are still among us, operating in a new department.

I do not wish to enlarge upon this topic, since it has already been amply discussed by Jonathan Swift and Mark Twain, among others. Let us just summarize the matter by saying that stupidity has murdered and imprisoned more geniuses, burned more books, slaughtered more populations, and blocked progress more effectively than any other force in history. It may be no exaggeration to say that stupidity has killed more people than all diseases known to medicine and psychiatry.

Various cures have been attempted, of course. Socrates thought he had found the cure in dialectic, Aristotle in logic, Bacon in experimental method, the eighteenth century in universal democracy and literacy, Freud in psychoanalysis, Korzybski in General Semantics, etc. Although all these inventions have been beneficial to some of us some of the time, they have not stopped the worldwide ravages of the plague, and they have not even abolished totally the occasional lapses into stupidity of their most accomplished practitioners (the present author emphatically included).

Stupidity is a contagious sociosemantic disturbance which afflicts all of us.

Stupidity murders geniuses, burns books, slaughters populations, blocks progress.

There is nothing rationally desirable that cannot be achieved if rationality itself increases.

Neurochemistry means the human nervous system studying and improving itself: intelligence studying and improving intelligence.

Why be depressed, dumb, and agitated when you can be happy, smart, and tranquil?

5

2. If intelligence could be increased, obviously solutions could be found more quickly to the various Doomsday scenarios presently threatening us.

(A) For instance, if each scientist working on the energy-resources problem could increase his or her intelligence by a factor of two, work that would otherwise require ten years could be accomplished in five.

(B) If human stupidity in general decreased, there would be less opposition to original thinking and to new approaches to our old problems.

(C) If stupidity decreased, less money would be wasted on vast organized imbecilities, such as the arms race, and more would be available for life-enhancing projects.

The same arguments apply to any other worthwhile goals: abolition of starvation and poverty, finding cures for cancer or schizophrenia, etc. *There is nothing rationally desirable that cannot be achieved sooner if rationality itself increases.* This is virtually a tautology, yet we seldom consider the corollary: *Work to achieve higher intelligence is work to achieve all of our other goals.*

3. Although dialectic, logic, experimental method, "democracy," literacy, psychoanalysis, General Semantics, etc. have not stopped the world-round ravages of stupidity, they have created certain counterforces: some enclaves of (comparative) rationality in which humans function with (comparatively) less stupidity than is normal for this domesticated primate species. "We" as a species have learned a few things from each of these inventions.

Those who are skilled in dialectic will not be fooled by the empty rhetoric of the more vulgar demagogues. Logic protects some of us from the more absurd "intellectual" (or anti-intellectual) fads of the epoch in which we live. Experimental method has shown us how to avoid the pitfalls of purely abstract

logic and connect our theorizing with actuality.

Democracy and literacy have made these previous inventions at least potentially available to huge masses rather than to tiny elites, although it remains true that you can lead the horses' asses to wisdom but you can't make them think. Psychoanalysis has shown us why even the most "rational" can become subject to compulsively irrational thinking. General Semantics has demonstrated the neurolinguistic reflexes that make it so difficult for humans to abandon an old model and accept a new one, and offers a few gimmicks that are somewhat helpful in breaking such reflexes.

But psychology has advanced quite a bit since Freud, psychoneurology since Korzybski, and Behavior Mod since Pavlov. We are on the threshold of a major breakthrough in the war against stupidity, just as surely as we are on the edge of achieving Life Extension and Space Migration. The Intelligence Revolution may even prove to be more wide-ranging in its effects than the quantum jumps to space industry and longevity.

4. Dr. Nathan Kline, who could be called a conservative in the area of neuropharmacology (on a scale in which Dr. Timothy Leary is radical and the U.S. government reactionary), has predicted in his *Psychotropic Drugs in the Year 2000* that, within 20 years, we will have drugs to improve memory, drugs to erase unpleasant memories, drugs to increase or decrease any emotion, drugs to prolong or shorten childhood, drugs to foster or terminate mothering behavior, etc. It takes no imagination to see that such chemicals will allow us greater control over our own nervous systems than was ever possible in the past. Obviously, people will *use and abuse* these drugs in many ways, desirable and otherwise, but

the most intelligent will use them in the most intelligent way, i.e., to increase their own neurological freedom, to deprogram their irrational programs, and generally to expand their consciousness and increase their intelligence.

The potential for neurological revolution implicit in such psychopharmacological advances should be quite clear to anybody who has any acquaintance even with so primitive a psychedelic as LSD. (One of the least-known facts about LSD is that the longest single research project with that chemical in the U.S., at the Spring Grove Hospital in Maryland, showed an average 10 per cent intelligence increase for all subjects; see Stafford, *Psychedelics Encyclopedia.*)

Walter Bowart has documented at length, in his *Operation Mind Control,* that hypnosis plus neurochemicals is more effective than ordinary hypnosis; that Behavior Mod plus neurochemicals is more effective than ordinary Behavior Mod; and that any mind-altering technique is more effective with neurochemicals than without. Bowart's evidence is all drawn from the misuse or perversion of these techniques, in the Army and CIA research on brainwashing, but there is no reason why libertarian and humane persons cannot use such knowledge to *de*condition and *de*program rather than merely to recondition and reprogram. Safe and sane principles for such mind-expansion and intelligence-liberation are already given in such books as Dr. John Lilly's *Programming and Metaprogramming in the Human Biocomputer, Neuropolitics,* by Dr. Leary, and *LSD: The Problem-Solving Psychedelic,* by Stafford and Golightly. *Please note that these books deal only with mind-liberation via LSD, but we are here talking about chemicals much more precise and predictable.* (Please reread the last sentence.)

5. If psychopharmacology is beginning to offer us the chance to program, deprogram, and reprogram ourselves at will, we are entering a new stage of evolution. More than psychoanalysis or General Semantics or Transactional Analysis or est or whatever mind-altering techniques of the past one may like, neurochemistry represents a real quantum jump to a new level of freedom: the human nervous system studying and improving itself, intelligence studying and improving intelligence.

To be even more specific and definite about this, consider the October 1975 McGraw-Hill poll of scientific opinion about what advances can be expected before 2000. The majority of neuroscientists in that poll predicted specific drugs to permanently increase human intelligence (see *No More Dying,* by Kurzman and Gordon, p. 4). I have saved this for mention *after* the more general Kline predictions to avoid the impression that I am talking *only* about the increase of third-circuit linear I.Q. There are seven other kinds of intelligence.

6. There is a direct feedback loop between psychopharmacology and the other brain sciences, such as electrical stimulation of the brain (ESB) and biofeedback, etc. As William S. Burroughs says, "Anything that can be done chemically can be done by other means." Jean Millay and others have demonstrated that yoga plus biofeedback produces detachment from imprinted emotional-perceptual sets much quicker than yoga alone. John Lilly has duplicated LSD effects with his isolation tanks. Jose Delgado has produced with ESB many effects previously found only with drugs.

It is commonplace for alarmists to warn us that the full armory of synergetically interacting neurosciences now evolving will allow unscrupulous governments to brainwash whole populations more totally than

7

ever before. We need to realize that the same technology, wisely used by intelligent men and women, can free us from every form of neurotic and irrational rigidity, allow us to dial and focus our nervous systems as easily as we dial or focus a TV set, turning any circuit on or off as we choose.

Why be depressed when you can be happy, dumb when you can be smart, agitated when you can be tranquil? Obviously most people are depressed, dumb, and agitated most of the time because *they lack the tools* to repair and correct damaged, defective circuits in their nervous systems. The Neurological Revolution (chemical, elec-

trical, biofeedback, and other) is giving us those tools. This HEAD Revolution has the Pleasure Principle to fuel it. That is, the more internal freedom you achieve, the more you want; it is more fun to be happy than sad, more enjoyable to choose your own emotions than to have them inflicted on you by mechanical glandular processes, more pleasurable to solve your problems than to be stuck with them forever.

In other words, Intelligence Increase basically means intelligence-studying-intelligence, and the first thing intelligence-studying-intelligence discovers is that the more intelligent you become, the more fun

Drugs to erase unpleasant memories, drugs to increase or decrease any emotion, drugs to prolong or shorten childhood, drugs to foster or terminate mothering behavior.

it is to try to become even more intelligent. (Which is just another way of saying that, neurologically at least, the more freedom you achieve, the more fun it is to work for even greater freedom.) Nobody is more interesting to anybody than is that mysterious character we all call "me," which is why self-liberation, self-actualization, self-transcendence, etc., are the most exciting games in town. This hedonic feedback explains why anybody who has taken even one step down the path toward neurological freedom can never be content to stop there, but is drawn on to the next step, and the next, forever—or as long as Life Extension can give us of forever.

7. In summary, Intelligence Increase is desirable, because every single problem confronting humanity is either directly caused or considerably worsened by the prevailing stupidity of the species; it is attainable, because modern advances in chemical, electrical, and other forms of brain change are showing us how to alter any imprinted, conditioned, or learned reflex that previously restricted us; it is hedonic, because the more freedom and intelligence you achieve, the more you see the advantages in seeking even more freedom and even more intelligence. It can accelerate our progress toward Space Migration and Life Extension, and toward any other rational goals, by creating more rationality to work on those goals; and it can

give us the wisdom to avoid the "bad" results of Life Extension and Space Migration that conservatives warn us about.

Like death and poverty, stupidity has been around so long that most people cannot imagine human life without it, but it is rapidly becoming obsolete. However many special-interest groups (politicians, clergy, advertisers, etc.) may profit from stupidity, humanity as a whole will profit more from its abolition. From here on, we should measure our progress toward our personal goals, and our contribution to humanity's world-round progress, in terms of how much smarter we have gotten in the last year, the last month, the last week, THE LAST HOUR.

HAGBARD CELINE was trained in contract law and naval engineering but claims he acquired his real education playing the piano in a whorehouse. He is captain of the world's largest submarine, the Leif Erikson, *and president of Gold and Appel Inc., an import-export firm that has frequently aroused the suspicions of law enforcement agencies ("137 arrests and no convictions," Hagbard brags). Some claim that he is a master of disguise and has successfully passed himself off under such alternative identities as Howard Cork, Hugh Crane, Captain Nemo, etc., and has appeared in countless epics and sagas.*

Neophobia/Neophilia Quiz

The following quiz, created by Illuminati International in collaboration with neuroanthropologist Blake Williams, measures one's capacity to participate in the HEAD Revolution. Answers are on page 30.

1. Add the next term to the series:
   (a) walk;
   (b) ride horseback;
   (c) fly by jet;
   (d) ——————— .

2. A certain job can be performed either by a human or a machine. We should
   (a) employ the human because "the devil makes work for idle hands."
   (b) employ the human because otherwise he or she might be bored.
   (c) employ the human because there is no way to organize society except by having most people work for wages.
   (d) employ the machine because technology has no other function than to free people from toil.

3. Add the next term to the series:
   (a) hunt and gather;
   (b) farm;
   (c) industry-commerce;
   (d) ——————— .

4. There is a magic machine with two buttons, each of which will create equality among humans. You will push

   (a) the button that makes everybody equally poor;
   (b) the button that makes everybody equally rich.

5. Add the next term to the series:
   (a) stone tablet;
   (b) ink and paper;
   (c) global TV;
   (d) ——————— .

6. Working for wages
   (a) has always existed and always will exist;
   (b) is ordained by God
   (c) did not appear on large scale until the Enclosure Acts drove the serfs off the land in the past 300 years;
   (d) will become obsolete in the next 100 years;
   (e) will become obsolete in the next 10 years.

7. Add the next term to the series:
   (a) numbers;
   (b) calendars;
   (c) scientific laws;
   (d) ——————— .

8. There are more scientists alive today than in all previous history. Toffler, among others, says this means we will have more changes in the next 30 years than in all previous history. We should therefore:
   (a) force half or more of the scientists to

become shoe clerks or grocers so things don't change too fast;

(b) establish a government committee to supervise all scientific research, thereby slowing it down even more;

(c) learn to raise general intelligence to cope with change.

9. The best way to search for Higher Intelligence is to

(a) find the right religion;

(b) support Carl Sagan's Project Cyclops, which is searching for radio signals from advanced civilizations in the galaxy;

(c) investigate UFOs;

(d) research our own nervous systems;

(e) build a starship and go looking.

10. Add the next term to the series:

(a) egocentric;

(b) chauvinistic;

(c) terracentric;

(d) _____ .

11. *Time* magazine says that "within 15 years" we will have the techniques to change our nervous systems for perpetual bliss.

(a) This is horrible; we'll all be destroyed by hedonism.

(b) This is fine; what else is neurological research good for?

(c) We've had the techniques since 1960, but imprisonment and harassment has silenced those who know about them.

12. Add the next term to the series:

(a) Black Pride;

(b) Women's Lib;

(c) Gay Lib;

(d) _____ .

13. Who do you believe:

(a) conservative authorities who say life-span will never increase much more than at present?

(b) Gerontologist Paul Segall, who says we can have 500-year lifespans?

(c) Biologist Johan Bjorkstein, who says we can have 800 years?

(d) Robert Phedra, M.D., who says we can have 1,000 years?

(e) Physicist R. C. W. Ettinger, who says we can have immortality?

14. The accepted opinions of today will seem quaint and somewhat inaccurate by:

(a) 2000;

(b) 2050;

(c) 2100.

15. The accepted opinions of today will appear to be idiotic superstitions by:

(a) 1986;

(b) 2000;

(c) 2100;

(d) 3000.

16. Add the next term to the series:

(a) non-Euclidean geometry;

(b) non-Newtonian physics;

(c) non-Aristotelian logic;

(d) _____ .

Courage is a habit like any other. So is cowardice.

Less than thirty years ago it was believed by many intellectuals that the United States was a matriarchy. The intellectuals who believed this were all males, but I don't know any other explanation for them.

The most intelligent book on
contemporary American politics,
I think, is Carl Oglesby's *The
Yankee and Cowboy War*; and yet
the whole book pivots on an
enormous fallacy. What the
Cowboys (Western money, as
distinguished from the Yankee
Establishment) do not understand,
Oglesby solemnly informs us, is
that "there is no more frontier."
He sounds like a very narrow
European writing in 1491; except
that our Columbus has already
sailed — our Columbuses, rather,
since there have been over 100 of
them. I wonder how many of the
Cowboys can see the High
Frontier invisible to Oglesby? And
I wonder if Oglesby has investi-
gated how much Cowboy wealth is
invested in space industry?

Bad critics judge a work of art
by comparing it to preexisting
theories. They always go wrong
when confronted with a master-
piece, because masterpieces make
their own rules.

12

𝔍tem

A Few of the Things I Know about Her

by Simon Moon

I know that She forever grows more lovable as I understand Her better; and that She forever grows more understandable as I love Her better.

I know that She is incarnate, a living presence, Anna Livia Plurabella, in every living creature of us, including the people I can't stand—which shows Her incredible humility, and Her fantastic sense of humor.

I know that She has time and time again ravished me entirely with Her beauty, so She is the supreme artist; and I know that She forever transcends my understanding, so She is the supreme intelligence; but She is more than beauty and intelligence.

I know that She inspires the Bard who sings to me, and that he is Her priest; and that I am only the local transmitter through which he broadcasts his eternal adoration for Her.

And I know that I adore Her, my Babalon! I adore Her, my dark-eyed Nu!

I know that it is the supreme glory of my life that She has manifested Herself to me, sometimes for hours on end, once even for two weeks; but She has manifested herself most truly in those brief moments when I have been annihilated entirely in Her.

I know that I can love Her best through one woman; but this is my nature, as a Capricorn, and there are other paths for other lovers of Her.

I know that, although She seems fickle and arbitrary at times, She is only so in my narrow egotistic view of things at the moment; and that I have understood Her, and loved Her, best in those moments when I accepted Her total perfection without question.

I know that She is my complement, my other Self; and that She is all the fiery intoxication that draws me out of my narrow self into eternal striving toward Her perfection.

And I know that I adore Her, my Babalon! I adore Her, my lion-loined Nu!

I know that I only know a few things about Her now, but I am lucky beyond belief, for once I knew nothing about Her.

I know that She loves me with as fierce a passion as I love Her; but She is promiscuous and loves all Her lovers that way.

I know that She is in the stars and between them; and in every sentient mind.

I know that all Her lovers go mad, by the judgment of this world; but this is false, for it is the world that is mad, and deranged, and besotted in grief—because it does not know Her.

And I know that I adore Her, my Babalon! I adore Her, my mother Nu!

I know that She is beyond metaphor, beyond speech, beyond thought; but She is radiantly sane and simple in Her heart.

I know that She is happiest of all, because She loves All; and She is wisest, because

She is drunken in Her ecstasy of creation.

I know that She is in the dance, because She is dance; but She is in the movements of the stars and in the astronomer's equations, for She is the Mother, not the Daughter, of Order.

I know that She is feared and comes as the nightmare into the minds of those who are without love; but She is forever gracious to those who sing to Her, and cry out to Her, and moan to Her, and repeat endlessly in their hearts:

I know that I adore Her, my Babalon! I adore Her, my soft-fleshed Nu!

I know that even though my heart may sing with the ecstasy of Her, and my brain whirl with the mystery of Her, one part of me will live in misery forever, until I am entirely lost in Her.

I know that even though my heart may sink with despair, and my brain stop with confusion, one part of me will be joyfully understanding forever, because I am not truly separate from Her.

I know that She is beyond intelligence, beyond emotion, beyond intuition; I know that She is drawing me beyond intelligence, beyond emotion, beyond intuition.

I know that I am enslaved and enraptured and destroyed by Her again and again and again until my words die in my throat and I can only moan as I try to repeat:

I adore Her, my Babalon! I adore Her, my hot-tongued Nu!

Llewellyn Publications, P.O. Box 43383, St. Paul, MN 55164 from GNOSTICA, September/October, 1975.

THE PARANOIDS ARE RIGHT: THEY'VE GOT LOTS OF ENEMIES
(Who would want to be their friends?)

Quantum Mechanics as a Branch of Primate Psychology

by Simon Moon

A ccording to the Copenhagen Interpretation
invented in the middle of the Carlsberg
  brewery 1926
by Niels Bohr
the world-as-known-to-science
is not a model of
the real world
but is—at one step remove—
a model of the human mind
building a model of
the real world.
The science of sciences, then,
THE SCIENCE, the fountainhead,
becomes epistemology,
which is a branch of human psychology,
which is a branch of primate psychology
and of
primate neurology.
The primate genetic imperatives
  of territoriality,
pack hierarchy,
rage-threat reflexes,
rule by an alpha male,
all play a role in

the theorizing/modeling of
domesticated primates
like us.
Or, as Eddington said,
"We have certain preconceived notions
of location in space
that have come down to us from
ape-like ancestors."
Get into your brain,
into the Jungian "collective unconscious,"
the DNA archives,
to find the origin of
philosophy, art, and
modern physics including
the Copenhagen Interpretation.

But
according to David Bohm 1952
the quantum jump is
controlled by a subquantum
hidden variable
which is nonlocal:
here, there, and everywhere in space:
now, then, and everywhen in time.
If Bohm is right,
the primate brain
(which devised *Lear* and
Beethoven's *Ninth* and
tic-tac-toe along with

quantum mechanics)
is the product of
DNA architectural design
to terraform Terra
which is dependent upon
quantum bonding of the DNA helix
which, in turn, is determined by
quantum jumpiness
determined itself by
the hidden variable
nonlocal in spacetime
omniscient, omnipotent, and omnipresent
as any theologian's God.

If Bohr is right,
the primary study is that of
the brain and consciousness
(primate neurology);
but if Bohm is right
the primary study is that of
the hidden variable
nonlocal in spacetime
(cosmic organization:
negative entropy, inc.)

Since Bohr himself said
"The opposite of a trivial truth
is false; the opposite of a great truth
is also true,"
we can synthesize Bohr/Bohm
and conclude that
primate neurology = the hidden variable
which in prescientific language
would read
the soul = God
except that to be true to Bohm
and to Bell's Theorem 1964
primate neurology (the soul)
also = any other point-event
which has a view of
the universe as accurate as
that of any other point-event
so that if the
hidden variable = God

so does the lampshade
or the blue spruce
(which is what any Buddhist
or acid-head will tell you
even without studying
quantum mechanics).

SIMON MOON is a second-generation anarchist and holds advanced degrees in mathematics and computer science. Moon consumes gargantuan quantities of pot, hash, acid and peyote, bragging that he hasn't "had an unhallucinated day since 1968." Easy to arouse, he is hard to pacify and most people prefer to just go away. "Bucky Fuller says he seems to be a verb," he told our interviewer, "but I am definitely a gerund." He lists his qualifications for membership in the Illuminati as fifty-five experiences of ESP, five hundred fifty-five demonstrations of PK, one out-of-book experience, and 2,317 synchronicities.

Conservatives say it is dangerous to give any group too much political power. Liberals say it is dangerous to give any group too much economic power. Both are right.

Dissociation of Ideas, 1

The term "dissociation of ideas" was coined by the French philosopher Remy de Gourmont, based on the Pavlovian discovery that the brain usually works in conditioned or habitual associations. To become more conscious and intelligent, de Gourmont proposed, examine all your habitual associations and try negating them.

For instance, if you mechanically associate technology with badness, try making a list of ten inventions that you really would not want to do without, starting with the printing press that brought you this intriguing experiment. Then add ten more. By then your dislike for technology should be somewhat less all-inclusive and more reasoned.

On the other hand, if you robotically associate technology with goodness, make a similar list of 20 things we could damned well do without, starting with the hydrogen bomb. Your allegiance to technology should then be somewhat more conscious and less mechanical.

Try the excercise every day, testing a new association each time. After all, the Sufis say if you can live even ten minutes without conditioned reactions, you are Illuminated.

Item

The Eight Circuits of the Nervous System

I.   The Terrestrial Circuits.

1. *The Biosurvival Circuit:* imprinted in infancy. Concerned with sucking, nourishment, cuddling, biosecurity.

2. *The Emotional-Territorial Circuit:* imprinted in the toddling stage. Concerned with territorial demands, emotional power tactics, political domination-and-submission strategies.

3. *The Semantic Circuit:* imprinted by human artifacts and symbol systems. Concerned with handling the environment, invention, calculation, prediction, building a "map" of the universe.

4. *The Sociosexual Circuit:* imprinted by the first orgasm-mating experiences and tribal "morals." Concerned with sexual pleasure, local definitions of "moral" and "immoral," reproduction, nurture of the young.

II. The Extraterrestrial Circuits.

5. *The Neurosomatic Circuit:* imprinted by ecstatic experience via physiological or chemical yogas. Concerned with neurological-somatic feedbacks, feeling high, somatic reprogramming (Christian Science, faith healing, etc.).

6. *The Metaprogramming Circuit:* imprinted by advanced yogas. Concerned with reimprinting and reprogramming all earlier circuits, relativity of "realities" perceived, cybernetic consciousness.

7. *The Neurogenetic Circuit:* imprinted by advanced yogas. Concerned with evolutionary consciousness (past and future), DNA-RNA-brain feedbacks, Jung's "Collective Unconscious."

8. *The Neuroatomic Circuit:* imprinted by shock or near-death experience. Concerned with quantum consciousness, non-local awareness (beyond spacetime), so-called "PSI" or "magick" powers, Illumination.

Adapted from *Exo-Psychology*, by Timothy Leary

Help conquer the IQ shortage: worry less and think more.

Conspiracy

Digest

Interview 1

CD: How seriously are we to take your fascinating and entertaining trilogy, Illuminatus!, which you wrote in collaboration with Robert J. Shea?

Wilson: I would hate to be taken seriously. Serious people are always so grim and uptight that they make me want to dance naked on the lawn playing a flute. Of course, as Mavis says in the first volume of the trilogy, nothing is true unless it makes you laugh, but you don't really understand it until it makes you cry. The basic situation of humanity is both tragic and comic, since we are all domesticated apes with marvelous 30-billion-cell brains, which we seldom use efficiently because of domination by the older mammalian parts of the back brain. I mean, we're living on the Planet of the Apes, man. Is that funny or serious? It depends on how broad your sense of humor is, I guess.

CD: Specifically, are we really to believe that competing secret societies initiate and guide the various intellectual, religious, artistic, and mind-warping trends of the world? Or was the secret-society scenario just a parody of right-wing theories, a way

of dramatizing authoritarian vs. libertarian trends, or simply your own brainwashing technique?

Wilson: To quote Lichtenberg, "This book is a mirror. When a monkey looks in, no philosopher looks out." Illuminatus!, like Linda Lovelace, is all things to all men. It's the first novel deliberately written from the viewpoint of the multi-model agnosticism of modern quantum physics. The novelist sitting on a pedestal watching the world with the allegedly Objective Eye of God is as obsolete as the tinhorn preacher bawling, "Come to my church, I've got the true true religion." The only philosophy one can honestly embrace at this stage of evolution is agnosticism, or ontological pluralism. The mosaic of competing conspiracies in Illuminatus! is a parody of popular demonology on both Right and Left. It's also a serious proposal for a more Einsteinian, relativistic model than the monistic Newtonian theories most conspiracy buffs favor. One of the readers who really seems to have understood Illuminatus! is Dr. Timothy Leary, who told me last year that his experiences with the DEA, FBI, CIA, PLO, Weather Underground, Mansonoids, Aryan Brotherhood, Al Fattah, etc., were precisely like the most absurd parts of Illuminatus! Tim says you meet the same 24 conspiracies wherever you go. Specifically, he mentioned that he identified the same 24 palaeolithic gangs fighting over the turf in Folsom Prison that he had recognized at Harvard University. The ones at Harvard speak better English, of course.

CD: How do you react to my theory that religious cults and secret societies are not prime movers, but simply pawns in the hands of amoral, Stirnerite International Bankers? As I recall, you hint in Illumi-

natus! that the International Bankers are controlled by the Illuminati.

Wilson: In the first place, I'm delighted that you call your scenario a theory and don't insist it's a proven fact. That raises you several degrees higher on the intelligence scale than most conspiracy buffs, who appear never to have studied logic, semantics, epistemology, or scientific method. They think that any wild idea that enters their heads must be true because it makes them feel even more terrified than they were yesterday. You see, most conspiracy buffs are adrenalin freaks and really get off on frightening the blue daylights out of themselves (and others). This is the same weird imprint that makes people go to sadistic horror movies.

Second, I think your theory is as plausible as my theory—or six or seven other theories. In general, however, I doubt very much that the International Bankers, or any other gang of pirates, knows what the hell is going on. Like every other conspiracy, they like to imagine they're really on top of everything, but that's just ego-tripping. As I point out in the Snafu Principle in volume two of *Illuminatus!, communication is only possible between equals.* Every hierarchy is a communication jam. Every ruling elite suffers from Progressive Disorientation: the longer they rule, the crazier they get. That's because everybody lies to the men in power—some to escape punishment, some to flatter and curry favor. The result is that the elite get a very warped idea of the world indeed. This applies to all pyramidal organizations—armies, corporations, or governments. It even applies to old-fashioned patriarchal families. The individual or group at the top feed entirely on flattering and deceptive garbage (the Howard Hughes syndrome). Gloriosky, the

tales I could tell about corporations where I've worked . . . such things are only possible on the Planet of the Apes.

Anyhow, the bankers are only part of a much bigger and stupider game, in which dozens of coalitions are plotting and scheming to deceive and rip off the others. The best model for understanding capitalist coalitions is Von Neumann and Morgenstern's *Theory of Games and Economic Behavior,* which points out that every coalition attempts to hide or hoard important signals. (Information, like everything else, becomes a commodity in capitalism, and typical mammalian hoarding behavior sets in. The more secrets a coalition has, the more important they think they are.) Intelligence depends on rapid exchange of signals, unfortunately for conspirators, so the hoarding of signals ("Top Secret," "Your Eyes Only," etc.) and the broadcasting of false signals (the politics of lying) reduce the IQ of those who are doing it even more catastrophically than the general intelligence of the whole society. Progressive Disorientation, as I called it before, is the ultimate fate of all conspiratorial systems. That's why Dr. Leary has the slogan "No More Secrets" for the Starseed Group—a coalition which is attempting a triple mutation in this generation, namely Space Migration plus Intelligence Increase plus Life Extension. (SMI^{2}LE, in Leary's convenient abbreviation.) *Secrets are more dangerous to those who hoard them than to those excluded.* Of course, Gandhi and Martin Luther King, Jr., understood this before Leary and always told the opposition in advance exactly *what* they were going to do and *where* and *when* and *why.* That's the only way to end the paranoia that infests this planet and to get out of the mammalian territorial game into a more human and rational game.

Taxation is robbery, based on monopoly of weapons.

Rent is the daughter of taxation, the taxation of land by private groups, based on monopoly of land.

Interest is the son of rent, the rent of money, based on monopoly of coinage.

In the "free market," competition would drive price down to the level of cost (approximately).

In monopoly capitalism, price always equals at least cost plus taxation plus rent plus interest.

Monopoly capitalism is not a free market.

I also think the conspiratorial element in banking should not be *over*stressed, for two reasons. First, of course, it has been impossible to talk about bankers' conspiracies since the 1930s without most of your audience thinking you are a Nazi or, at least, an anti-Semite. This is what is called a conditioned association, or uncritical inference, and, however illogical it is, it is very widespread. I've been attacking the bankers since about 1962, and I never stop getting mail from two groups of idiots: Jewish idiots who think I'm secretly an anti-Semite, and are angry at me for it; and anti-Semitic idiots who also think I'm a secret anti-Semite, and are glad to welcome me to their loathsome club. (Of course, what makes this "anti-banker" = "anti-Jew" equation totally absurd is that the biggest banks in America today are controlled by old New England Protestant families—the "Yankees" in Carl Oglesby's quite plausible "Cowboys vs. Yankees" scenario, which holds that these Yankees are in a life-and-death struggle with Texas oilmen and other Western coalitions.)

Second, and more important, I am convinced that the problem in our banking system is *structural*, not personal. That is, if Jesus and his 12 apostles took over the Federal Reserve tomorrow, but were not allowed to change the rules, the Fed would still be a monstrosity. In other words, it doesn't matter who the players are. It is the game itself, the monopoly on issue of currency, that is the problem.

Of course, none of this is meant to deny that the bankers *do* conspire—just as the oil people conspire, or the marijuana smugglers, or the cliques who run the art world, etc. As Adam Smith said 200 years ago, "Men of the same profession never gather together except to conspire against the general public."

I see the power game as resting on three levels of force and fraud. First, earliest and still most powerful is the government racket itself, the *monopoly on force* (military power, police power, etc.) which allows the governing group to take tribute (taxation) from the enslaved or deluded masses. Second, derivative from this primordial conquest, is the landlord racket, *the mammalian monopoly on territory* which allows the king's relatives (lords-of-the-land) or their successors, today's "land-lords," to take tribute (rent) from those who live within the territory. Rent is the daughter of taxation; the second degree of the same racket. Third, the latest in historical time, is the usury racket, *the monopoly on the issue of currency* which allows the money-lords to take tribute (interest) on the creation of money or credit, and on the continuous circulation of the money or credit every step of the way. Interest is the son of rent, the rent of money. Since most people engaged in nefarious practices are, in my opinion and contrary to your model, very loathe to acknowledge what they are doing, and are addicted to the same hypocrisies as the rest of humanity, I think all power groups quite sincerely believe that what they are doing is proper, and that anybody who attacks them is a revolutionary nut. Outside of the Klingons on *Star Trek*, I have never encountered a real predator who justifies himself on Stirnerite or Machiavellian grounds. I really think Saroyan was right, naive as it sounds, in saying that "every man is a good man in his own eyes."

Specifically, I don't think Rockefeller and his friends talk among themselves like old-fashioned stage villains, gloating over how they're "duping" and "exploiting" the rest of us (as you portray them in your *Occult Technology of Power*, otherwise an excellent book). They talk about "maintaining the civilized order," like the professor who works for them in the Council on Foreign Relations scene in *Illuminatus!* That's the kind of jargon used by Carroll Quigley, the one Establishment historian who really gave away the show; and in the Trilateral Commission report, *The Crises in Democracy*, you find the same self-flattering image. This is hardly surprising. All the other coalitions and conspiracies think of themselves as the Good Guys, too. Everybody thinks the competition or the insurrectionary forces are the Bad Guys.

CD: While it may be true that conspiracy buffs are "adrenalin freaks," isn't it also true that the much more common and respectable "trusting souls" are self-pacifiers who are afraid to consider frightening theories of reality, regardless of evidence?

Wilson: Certainly! The first circuit of the nervous system, the infantile biosurvival imprint, tends to produce a robotic pro-

The brain is the greatest sex organ of all.

gram of trust-dependency-optimism or of suspicion-fear-withdrawal, and this usually remains constant for life. Both extremes of this imprint are quite mechanical. *Illuminatus!* is an ontological hotfoot, intended to provoke some real cortical activity in place of these robot imprints.

CD: It seems obvious that most people are biased in the self-calming direction, and that this complacent attitude plays right into the hands of conspirators in business and government. Comment?

Wilson: Perhaps we *are* talking about different planets. My experience is that almost everybody thinks *somebody else* is to blame for their problems. If it isn't the Jews or the Catholics or the International Bankers, it's the Masons or the ecologists or the local utility. Kids blame their parents. Parents blame their kids. In a sense, all of these "conspiracy" theories are self-calming, in that they put the problem outside in an "enemy" who can be hated and blamed, but that is the only sense in which I find the average domesticated primate to be self-calming. To organize a lynch mob or a riot—to yell, "The Enemy's over there, fellers!" and get a crowd behind you—is still the easiest game on the Planet of the Apes. The most important passage in *Illuminatus!*, to me, is the "Now Look What You Made Me Do" fable by the Dealy Lama (which is now a rock song in the English stage version of *Illuminatus!*) and that's the real moral of the trilogy. We can only be sane and responsible if we stop looking *outside* ourselves for strength (Big Daddy or God) or for somebody to blame (The Devil). God and Devil are real, but *inside* us.

Of course, I got the idea for "Now Look What You Made Me Do" from Laurel and Hardy. I forget which of their movies it was

in, but I remember Hardy, after some disaster, turning to Laurel and saying, "Now look what you made me do." It hit me in a flash that, like all great moments in comedy, this was a profound epiphany in the Joycean sense, a synecdoche of how people always try to blame somebody else for their own behavior.

Preceding was written in 1976; following was written in 1979.

The difference between me and *Conspiracy Digest* is that *CD* defines the Power Elite as somebody else. I always define the Power Elite as myself and my friends.

CD and I are in basic agreement that certain kinds of power are vested in: (a) those who monopolize weaponry, i.e., governments; (b) those who monopolize land, i.e., landlords; and (c) those who monopolize currency, i.e., banks of issue. We disagree in that *CD* regards these traditional monopolies as possessing the only kind of power that matters on this planet; and I recognize another kind of power, Brain power.

Brain power (the work of all artists, scientists, and symbolizers since the dawn of humanity, but particularly those of the nineteenth century) created the "real world" over which monopolists fight each other in the twentieth century. Similarly, Brain power right now, today, is creating the "real world" of the twenty-first century, over which the monopolies will then be struggling. The Brain people create the realities over which the Power people fight each other, and the Brain people even create the techniques of the fight.

Specifically, World War III has been prevented by one Primus Illuminatus named John Von Neumann, already mentioned in connection with his quantum-mechanics work and his theory of games. Von Neumann also designed the first programmable computer, which he whimsically named MANIAC (Multiple Analyzer Numerical Integrator And Computer). When militarists everywhere began using programmable (post–Von Neumann) computers and the Von Neumann game theory to analyze "war games," they quickly learned that nuclear war is a no-win situation. Their own strategists, examining possible war scenarios with Von Neumann's math in Von Neumann's computers, were forced to realize that thermonuclear showdown was unwinnable; hence, traditional power politics now operates with cold wars, bush wars like Vietnam, wars of intelligence agencies against intelligence agencies, etc., but not with World Wars.

The same Brain power can create a twenty-first century in which the power struggles will be, perforce, intelligence struggles, and no violence will be possible.

ROBERT ANTON WILSON is an imaginary being created by God. Since he is fairly bright, Wilson has figured this out and knows he has no real existence aside from the mind of God. Nonetheless, he still relapses into taking himself seriously on occasion.

We're living on the Planet of the Apes. Is that funny or serious?

Neuroeconomics

by Hagbard Celine

S ociety derives from sex, from reproductive relationships. Mammalian pair bonds and pack bonds (imprinted emotions of affection and trust) held the first human bands and tribes together as working units. At the center, the hub, stood the orgasmic tenderness—the shared love of the genital embrace in the mating act—and out of this radiated the "sublimated" tenderness of parent-infant, brother-sister, uncles and aunts and grandparents, the whole "extended family" or hunting/food-gathering band.

Society derives from sex, from mammalian pair bonds and pack bonds.

The conquering State, and the subsequent fission of society into separate classes of privileged and deprived, created poverty. Poverty as a human institution derives from conquest, from the establishment of government (the invading warrior band, remaining to rule that which they have conquered), and from the institution of "laws" to perpetuate the class division between Invaders and Invaded.

The human, like any other primate, contains neurogenetic circuits ready to be imprinted by pair bonds and pack bonds. The evolutionary purpose of these bonds remains classically mammalian: they insure biosurvival and pack status. They also program most of the seed with the heterosexual-reproductive behaviors necessary for the survival of the pack, which in turn provides biosurvival security for future generations.

The State, fissioning society into separate classes of the privileged and deprived, created poverty.

The rise of the conquering State, the feudal State, and eventually the modern capitalist State has progressively undermined and subverted the tribal pack bond (the "extended family"). In the most advanced capitalist nation, USA, little pack bonding remains. Hardly any US citizens will stop for hitchhikers, give to beggars on the street, or even trust their neighbors. Many don't even *know* their neighbors. Normal pack bonding behaviors of trust, charity, affection, etc., still found in the feudal nations, have atrophied here. The celebrated "anomie," "anxiety," "alienation," etc., of capitalist society begins from this lack of normal pack bonding.

The circuits which normally imprint a pack bond still survive, ethologically speaking. (In psychological language, the same thought would be expressed by saying that the need for biosurvival security still survives.) This mammalian constant must be satisfied, and in an abstract society the satisfaction becomes abstract.

Paper money becomes the biosurvival imprint in capitalist society.

Paper money becomes the biosurvival imprint in capitalist society.

William S. Burroughs has compared capitalism to heroin addiction, pointing out the terrible parallels: the junkie must have regular doses; the capitalist citizen must have a regular money fix. If junk is not available, the addict becomes a spasmodic bundle of anxieties; if money is not available, the capitalist citizen goes through similar withdrawal trauma. When junk becomes scarce, junkies behave desperately, and will steal or even kill. When money becomes scarce, capitalist citizens will also rob or kill.

Opiate drugs, according to Dr. Timothy Leary, function as biosurvival circuit neurotransmitters. That is, they activate neural networks keyed to the mother-infant bond. (In the terms of preneurological Freudian psychology, the junkie in the arms of Mother Opium regresses to infantile bliss.) In a society without the normal mammalian

pack bond, similar imprinting occurs on money, by conditioning learned associations onto the infantile reflexes. The capitalist citizen learns neurologically that *money equals security* and *lack of money equals insecurity.*

Infantile separation anxiety (the fear of losing the all-providing Mother) became generalized to tribal separation anxiety quite early in hominid evolution. The person thrown out of the tribe for deviant or antisocial behavior experienced *real* survival anxiety. (The tribe, in primitive conditions, has much greater survivability than the lone individual. Ostracism then usually meant death, just as ostracism from Mother can mean death to the infant.)

Since money has replaced the tribe in capitalist society, the majority of citizens have imprinted onto money the traditional mammalian emotions of the infant-mother and individual-pack survival bonds. This imprinting is maintained by conditioned associations created by real deprivation experience. Before the rise of welfarism, people did die of money withdrawal in capitalist society, in large numbers; and it still happens occasionally, among the very ignorant, the very timid, the very old. (E.g., an elderly couple froze to death in Buffalo, a few years ago, when they were unable to pay their utility bill and the local monopoly shut off their heat, in January.)

The frequent European observation that Americans "are money-mad" merely signifies that capitalist abstraction, and decline of the tribe, has advanced further here than in European capitalist states.

The American, deprived of money, lurches about like a frenzied lunatic. "Anxiety," "anomie," "alienation," etc., increase exponentially, reinforced by real security deprivations. The poor in less abstracted societies share a pack bond and "love" each other (on a village level). The poor in America, lacking the pack bond, hooked only on money itself, hate each other. This explains the paradoxical observation of many commentators that poverty retains dignity and even some pride in traditional societies, but appears dishonorable and shameful here. Indeed, the American poor not only hate each other; often, perhaps usually, they hate themselves.

The American, deprived of money, lurches about like a frenzied lunatic.

These facts of neuroeconomics have been so charged with pain and embarrassment that most Americans will not discuss them at all. The sexual prudery of the nineteenth century has become money prudery. People will talk, in the *avant* third of the population anyway, quite explicitly about the fetishistic aspects of their sex imprints ("I get off on wearing my wife's underwear during the foreplay," or whatnot), but equal frankness about our money needs freezes the conversation and may empty the room.

Behind superficial pain and embarrassment lies mammalian terror: biosurvival anxiety.

The mobility of modern society escalates this money-anxiety syndrome. During the 1930s depression, for instance, many grocers and other "corner stores" allowed customers to run up quite large bills, over periods of months sometimes. This was based on the last tattered fragments of the traditional tribal bond and the fact that everybody still knew everybody in the

neighborhoods of those days (40 years ago). Today, it would not happen. We live, as one novel said, in a "world full of strangers."

In the opening chapter of *The Confidence Man*, Melville contrasts the "religious nut" who carries a sign saying "LOVE ONE ANOTHER" with the merchants whose signs say, "NO CREDIT." The irony was meant to reflect on the uneasy mixture of Christianity and capitalism in nineteenth-century America—but Christianity, like Buddhism and the other posturban religions, appears to be largely an attempt to recreate the tribal bond on a mystical level within "civilized" (i.e., imperialist) times. Welfarism represents the State's attempt to counterfeit such a bond (in a stingy and paranoid fashion, in the spirit of capitalist law). Totalitarianism appears as the eruption, in murderous fury, of the same endeavor to convert the State into a tribal nexus of mutual trust and biosurvival support.

The dawn of libertarian philosophy in America featured two tendencies which modern libertarians have neglected—unwisely, if the above analysis proves sound. I refer to the emphasis on *voluntary association*—retribalization on a higher level, through shared evolutionary goals—and on *alternative currencies*. The former of these ideas appears prominently in Warren, Greene, Spooner and Tucker, among others; the latter in all the above and in Dana, Ingalls, C. L. Schwartz, Joseph Labadie, Bilgrim, Levy, etc.

Voluntary associations or communes without alternative currencies quickly become reabsorbed into the capitalist cash nexus. Voluntary associations with alternative currencies openly declared get ground up in the courts and destroyed. Voluntary associations using covert or secret currencies, as in *Illuminatus!*, may actually exist, to judge from hints or codes in some right-wing libertarian publications.

No form of libertarianism or anarchism (including anarchocapitalism and anarcho-communism) can successfully compete with welfarism or totalitarianism, under present conditions.

Current welfare practices emerged from 70 years of struggle between liberals and conservatives; the conservatives won most of the battles. The system functions to heighten the addiction syndrome. The recipient gets a small fix at the beginning of the month, nicely calculated to support one extremely frugal miser until about the 10th of the month. Through hard experience, he or she learns to make this last until the 15th, maybe even to the 20th. The rest of the month is experienced as acute biosurvival anxiety. This deprivation period, as any pusher or Skinnerian conditioner knows, maintains the whole cycle. On the first of the next month, another money fix is allowed, and the whole drama begins anew.

The welfare rolls steadily increase, since —even with the most bumbling inefficiency and redundancy—the tendency of industrialism remains, as Buckminster Fuller says, to do more with less and omniephemeralize. Each decade, fewer will have jobs and more will be on welfare. (Already, 0.5 per cent own 70 per cent of the wealth, leaving 99.5 per cent to compete violently for the remainder.) The end result could become a totally conditioned society, entirely abstract, motivated only by neurochemical money addiction.

To measure our advance toward that condition, imagine vividly what you would do and feel if all your money and sources of money disappeared tomorrow.

It is important to bear strongly in mind that we are still discussing *standard mammalian behaviors*. In recent research, chim-panzees have been trained to use money. The reports indicate that they developed normal "American" attitudes toward the mysteriously powerful tokens.

Each decade, fewer will have jobs and more will be on welfare.

The Illuminati pyramid on the dollar bill, like the similar "magick" emblems of the *Fleur de Lys*, Swastika, Two-Headed Eagle, Stars, Suns, Moons, etc., with which other nations have seen fit to festoon their State currencies or documents, is intrinsic to the "spookiness" of the whole monopolization of *mana* or psychic energy by the State. Here are two pieces of green paper; one is money, the other is not. The difference is that the former was "blessed" by the wizards in the Treasury Buidling.

The capitalist worker lives with the same perpetual anxiety as the opiate addict. The source of biosurvival security, the neuro-chemistry of feeling safe, is hooked to an external power. The conditioned chain *money equals security, no money equals terror,* is reinforced continually by seeing others "fired" and fallen by the wayside. Psychologically, this state may be categorized as *chronic low-grade paranoia*. Politically, the manifestation of this neurochemical imbalance is known as Fascism: the Archie Bunker/Adolph Schickelgruber/Richard Nixon mentality.

As Leary says, "Fear and rage restrictions on freedom now dominate our social life . . . fear and restricting violence can become addictive kicks, reinforced by schizophrenic policymakers and an economic system which depends upon restricting freedom, and upon the production of fear and the inciting of violent behavior."

In Desmond Morris's perfect metaphor, the naked ape behaves exactly like a zoo animal: despair is the essence of the cage experience. In our case, the bars are intangible, imprinted game-rules: Blake's "mind-forg'd manacles." *We are literally being robbed blind. We have literally taken leave of our senses.* The conditioned token, the symbol money, controls our mental well-being.

This appears to be what Norman O. Brown is groping to say in his occult-Freudian tomes about our "polymorphous perversity" (natural body rapture) being destroyed in the process of conditioning sublimated sex (group bonding) onto social games like money. The Resurrection of the Body that Brown foresees can only happen by means of neurosomatic mutation or, as Leary calls it, Hedonic engineering. Historically, the only groups that have managed to detach themselves effectively from the social game anxiety have been (1) absolutely secure aristocracies, free to explore the various "mental" and "physical" pleasures, and (2) communes of shared voluntary poverty, a form of retribalization by sheer determination.

Libertarians, like other idealists and malcontents of Left and Right, generally suffer a wounding sense of the ghastly chasm between their evolutionary goals and the present grim reality. This sense vastly complicates the resolution of their own money-anxiety syndrome, with the result that virtually all of them feel intense guilt about the ways they acquire the money necessary to survive in the domesticated-ape world around us.

"He has sold out," "She has sold out," "I

have sold out," are accusations heard daily in every idealistic clique.

Any way of "making money" automatically opens one to guilt-inducing vibrations from one faction, while it paradoxically spares one from further guilt-inducing vibrations from another faction. Catch-22, the Double Bind, the Snafu Principle, etc., are merely extensions of the basic neuro-economic trap: You Can't Live Without Money.

As Joseph Labadie concluded, "Poverty doth make cowards of us all."

"Poverty doth make cowards of us all."

There is, ultimately, a pleasure in *enduring* poverty. It is like the pleasure of surviving through grief and mourning and loss; the Hemingway pleasure of standing firm and continuing to fire at a charging lion; the saint's pleasure in forgiving those who persecute her. It is not masochism but pride: I have been stronger than I thought I could be. "I have not wept nor cried aloud." This is the joy Nietzsche and Gurdjieff found, in ignoring their cruelly painful illnesses and writing only of the "awakened" state beyond emotions and attachments.

Right-wing paranoia about paper money (the various conspiracy theories about how the supply and withdrawal of money is manipulated) will always remain epidemic in capitalist society. Junkies have similar myths about the pushers.

It is real food, real clothing, real shelter that are threatened when money is removed, even briefly, and it is real deprivation that occurs when money is removed for any length of time. The domesticated ape is trapped by a game of mental symbols, but the trap is deadly.

There is some kind of masochistic pleasure in continuing the analysis of a painful subject into every byway and intricacy of its labyrinthine torments. There is something of this beneath the "objectivity" of Marx, Veblen, Freud, Brooks Adams. "As bad as it is, we can at least look at it without screaming," such writers seem to be assuring us, and themselves.

"Only those who have drunk from the same cup know us," said Solzhenitsyn. He was talking about prison, not poverty, but the two are alike in being traditional punishments for dissent. One takes pride in having borne them, if one survives at all.

A popular opinion suggests that the counter-culture of the 1960s was beaten to death by cops' clubs, drug busts, other direct violence. My impression is that it was simply starved out. The money was cut off, and after sufficient deprivation the survivors crawled aboard the first capitalist life raft that was passing.

Capitalism, Jack London wrote, has its own heaven (wealth) and its own hell (poverty). "And the hell is real enough," he added, from bitter experience.

Fatherhood is problematical at best, but becomes a hero's task under capitalism. When the money supply is cut off, the father of a family in the USA today experiences multiplied anxiety: fear for self, fear for those who love and trust one. Only the captain of a sinking ship knows this vertigo, this wound.

To survive terror is the essence of true Initiation. For they live happiest who have forgiven most, and, as Nietzsche said, anything that doesn't kill me makes me stronger.

Originally published in No Governor *newsletter.*

Answers to Neophobia/Neophilia Quiz

There are no correct answers. The future depends on the decisions you and I make in the next hour, the next week, the next decade.

Dissociation of Ideas, 2

Distinguish between Feminism and Women's Liberation.

Feminism is, simply, a demand for justice which all ethical persons must support. It may be more basic than any other demand for justice, because the exploitation of women is damaging also to children and thereby to the whole human race; so that anybody who works for Feminism is working for the sanity of the species.

Women's Liberation is a specific brand of Feminism born out of the ugliness and fanaticism of New Left politics. To some extent, it has outgrown the worst aspects of that background; to some extent, it has not. It will outgrow that ugliness eventually, as the HEAD revolution teaches everybody to use their brains better. Meanwhile, one can support Feminism and still recognize that Women's Liberation, like all the fallout of the New Left, is partly a pathological hate trip.

Coex! Coex! Coex!

I've been reading/studying/reveling in *Finnegans Wake* for 32 years now; I started it at 16. Joyce said in one of his joking moods, "This will keep the professors busy for the next thousand years," and I believe him. I find new depths and profundities, and more jokes, every time I reread it.

For the historical record and as a politico-literary irony, it should be recorded that I was turned on to this great novel/symphony/jokebook/dream/myth/epic by James T. Farrell.

(Who? James T. Farrell was an influential and occasionally brilliant Marxist-realist of the 1930s and 1940s. His books became unfashionable when his politics became taboo. Farrell wasn't as good as the liberal-Marxoid critics of the '30s claimed, but he is good enough not to deserve the oblivion that has fallen upon him.)

Farrell had a defense of the *Wake* in one of his books of literary criticism. He said that Joyce's epic investigation of the mind of one man asleep was not devoid of social significance and that it was a perversion of Marxism to dismiss such work as irrelevant to the Revolution. I don't think Farrell convinced a single Marxist—most of them are still hostile to Joyce—but he convinced me. I bought the *Wake* on my 16th birthday, in 1948, started reading it, and haven't stopped yet.

Phil Gardner

sure is to learn to think with your *whole* brain, "conscious" and "unconscious" circuits included, in holistic *coex* systems.

Dr. Nick Herbert devised Diagram A to illustrate a possible "context-dependent language" which could describe modern quantum theory.

There are many good literary studies of Joyce, but the best introduction to *Finnegans Wake* is probably Dr. Stanislaus Grof's *Realms of the Human Unconscious*, a study of the head spaces experienced under LSD. In particular, Grof's term "*coex* systems" should be understood by everybody who writes about Joyce or tries to read him. A "*coex* system" is a *condensed experience montage*. E.g., you are reexperiencing the birth process, remembering prebirth interuterine events, reliving ancestral or archaeological crises of people/animals from whom you are descended, seeing the subatomic energy whorl from which Form appears, previsioning the Superhumanity of the future, and suffering horrible guilt over your unkindness to another child when you were four years old ... *all at once!*

Critics have tried to explain *Finnegans Wake* by means of Freud and Jung, but Joyce was a quantum jump ahead of the psychology of his time. Everything in *Finnegans Wake* is a *coex* system in Grof's sense. We can only understand it in terms of the latest findings in neurology, genetics, sociobiology, and exopsychology. To learn to read *Finnegans Wake* with ease and plea-

In such a language *A* would take its total meaning from the context of *B, C, D,* and *E; B,* in turn, would take its total meaning from *A, C, D,* and *E;* and so forth. This is also the way an LSD-induced *coex* system operates, and the way the great dream-myth of *Finnegans Wake* operates.

Example: the word "thuartpeatrick" on page 1 of the *Wake*. With the simultaneity of a *coex* system, this contains the following.

1. "Thou art Peter," the English version of the pun on which the Catholic Church is allegedly founded. (*Petrus* means rock, and Jesus' pun goes on "and on this Rock I will build my church.")

2. "Tu es Petrus," the Latin vulgate of the same phrase, superimposed upon the English.

3. A pun on "thwart," relating in the total context of the book to the sexual frustrations of the dreamer, H. C. Earwicker.

4. The "peat ricks" which used to stand beside every Irish home, providing fuel. This is one of a few dozen puns on the first page which help locate the dreamer in Ireland; others more specifically locate him in Dublin.

5. A pun on the Gaelic of "Patrick"

("Paidrig"), Ireland's national saint, another reinforcement of the Irish locale of the dream.

6. A pun on "pea trick," referring to the many other "pea" puns in the book, all revolving around the phrase "like as two peas in a pod" and referring to the fact that the dreamer's sons are twins, physically indistinguishable but psychologically opposite.

7. In context, a reference to the repeated refrain "mind your p's and q's," which refers to the dreamer's guilts generally, and, by the association of the sound of p and "pea," to "pee" and the dreamer's unconscious urinary obsession.

8. A suggestion that the Catholic Church, or *Finnegans Wake* itself, or maybe literature generally, is a "pea trick," or shell game, a semantic game in which words almost become the realities they symbolize.

This is not all there is in "thuartpeatrick," I'm sure; it's merely what I've gleaned in 30 or 40 readings of *Finnegans Wake*. Knowing Joyce's methods, I wouldn't be surprised if there are references to cannibalism in Lithuanian or to rivers in Russian also concealed in this word. (For instance, I was convinced for years that "the whiteboyce of Hoodie Head," also on page 1, concealed only the White Boys, an Irish revolutionary group of the nineteenth century, and the Ku Klux Klan, an American parallel. Then I learned that *Hode* in German is testicles, and realized the phrase signified the spermatozoa in the testicles.)

Another delightful example of Joyce's *coex* language is "goddinpotty," from Chapter Four. Here we can find the following superimposed upon each other.

1. *Garden party*. The speaker in this scene is an Englishwoman and Joyce is parodying English upperclass speech, in which "garden party" indeed sounds like "goddinpotty."

2. Garden party also suggests the Garden of Eden theme that runs all through the book (from the appearance of Eve and Adam in the first sentence) and, hence, the Fall of Man and, thus, in the same line of dream symbolism, the Fall of Finnegan from which the book takes its title.

3. The Fall of Man in the Garden of Eden links up with the dreamer's guilt about some mysterious "sin" he committed in the bushes in Phoenix Park, Dublin.

4. "God" and "din" suggest the thunder god, Thor, who is one of the principal characters in the dream—possibly because the thunder strikes ten times during the night.

5. God-in-potty suggests, to anyone raised Catholic, the Host in the chalice, the bread that becomes the Body of God when the priest speaks the magic formula over it.

6. But the dreamer himself is the Host, in two senses: (a) in waking life, he is Host of an inn; (b) throughout the dream, he is periodically denounced, condemned, executed, and devoured cannibalistically, and rises from the dead. This repeats the pattern of the Christ myth, just as the blessing and eating of the Host in the Mass does. It also repeats all the other dead-and-resurrected vegetation gods in Jung's collective unconscious. (In the Freudian personal unconscious, the trials and executions represent the dreamer's sexual guilts.)

7. "Potty" again brings in the dreamer's infantile urinary obsessions.

It will be observed that in analyzing only two phrases (three words) from the *Wake*, we have stumbled upon virtually every important theme of the dream, of the hero's personal unconscious, and of humanity's collective DNA archives. Joyce doesn't pack quite that much into every phrase, of course; but if you have found only two levels of reference in one of his puns, you have probably missed at least two others, and maybe as many as in these examples.

Finnegans Wake is not just a great novel and a semantic symphony; it contains a whole science of psychoarchaeology and historical neurolinguistics. As John Gard-

ner said of it, "Joyce dredged in that book. No other human being in the history of the world, including Beethoven, has ever given every single piece of emotion and thought and feeling the way Joyce did. He dredged up every ounce of his soul, every cell, every gene."

From: The Order of the Illuminati, Sirius Section To: Galactic Central

The progress of the domesticated primates of Terra has been advancing nicely since we introduced the Tarot deck five krals ago. As predicted, the amusement of the Tarot game has led to wide dispersion of the cards among the primates, and some have inevitably learned to use the cards also for scanning quantum probability waves and thus foreseeing "future" events. A few have even begun to decode the evolutionary script in the structure of the deck. We have, therefore, elected to introduce a second educational device among them, once again disguised as a game.

The new game is called "*chess.*" Detailed instructions for play, with a hologram of the playing board, are enclosed as an appendix to this report.

The purpose of the chess board is to insinuate a correct model of the primate brain into the semantic circuit of said brain, with the hope that, as with the Tarot, the smarter primates will gradually decipher it.

To begin with, we have made the board of black and white squares, although it can be altered to black and red, or any other starkly contrasting polarity, as suits the whims of various primate artisans. The essential signal will remain the same,

although black/white is, of course, the strongest artistic expression of the encoded symbolism.

The primal message is, as Your Lucidity will readily scan, the basic positive-negative (off-on) pulsation of all energy forms. Since we have already infiltrated this signal into Terran culture in several other artifacts and toys (see Memo 2317, "On the Chinese *Yin-Yang* and Related Electronic Codes"), the more intuitive primates will easily recognize its reiteration 32 times in the 64 squares of the chess board. We thus hope confidentially that some of them will eventually contemplate the relation between the eight rows of the board, the eight files, the proportions of 8 × 4 = 32 and 8 × 8 = 64, etc., thereby deducing the great Law of Octaves which we are still trying to teach them.

Since the chess board itself models the Terran brain, as they will gradually realize, the black-white symbolism will help them to intuit the relationship between the active left hemisphere (*Yang*) and the passive right hemisphere (*Yin*). As in all neurogenetic codes, we include extra information in each signal. Thus we hope the on-off (positive-negative) symbol will simultaneously suggest to them the on-off nature of consciousness itself (and the unreality of their current static self-images or egos); the off-on functioning of the individual synapse; the on-off of the emotional-glandular switches; the off-on of the sleep-waking cycle; etc.

We cheerfully predict that, within only a few tneks, some Terran primate gazing at a chess board will intuit "in a flash," as they say, that the repeated pattern of black-white-black-white-black-white-black-white, etc., is the peak and crest of a sine wave, entirely similar to their own + − + − + − + − brain processes. In short, a philosopher will arise among them to announce that the illusion of a continuous ego is caused by insufficient self-observation.*

To reiterate the basic application of the plus-minus polarity to the Terran brain, we have encoded the signal in a more complex and subtle way into the larger design of the chess board. That is, we have divided it into a seemingly strong "King side" and a seemingly weak "Queen side." We have also divided it (rather obviously) into a "strong" white side and a "weak" black side. The strength of the white side is so blatant, in fact, that the primates, as soon as we introduced the game, established a tradition to "make the game more fair." This tradition obliges the players to exchange roles, so

that whoever is white (has the advantage) in one game must play black (have the disadvantage) in another game.

This is where we get sneaky. Having discovered that one side of the board is stronger, going up the ranks, they will soon try to learn if one half is stronger, going across on the files. It will seem obvious to them that the "King" side (from white's perspective) is stronger. To make the neurological lesson obvious even to a Terran primate, *we have placed the "strong" King side where the right hand of the "strong" (white) player naturally rests.* Thus, each time primates play this "harmless game," they will be neurologically absorbing the information that the "strong" right hand is connected with the "King side" modes of thought, i.e., those in the left hemisphere of the brain (*Yang*).

It is our estimate that, given the dominance of right-hand, left-hemisphere functions in all primitive species at this stage of development, and given also the mode of male superiority that the primates of Terra have currently adopted, they will almost all try to win the game on the "King side." This is one of the jokers built into our code.

We estimate that it will take 1.5 krals before even the cleverest of the Terrans realizes that the "Queen side," corresponding to the left-hand, right-hemisphere neurological mode, is actually the stronger side. This lesson should have a dramatic "shock treatment" effect on their evolution.*

---

* *Addendum:* It happened within only two krals. The philosopher was named Gotama, and his disciples made a religion (Buddhism) out of his observations, garbling the transmission considerably. Within half a kral, however, another philosopher made the same observation; his name was David Hume, and most of the other philosophers are still busy trying to "refute" him. In only an eighth of a kral since then, a group of clever investigators named Maxwell, Faraday, Planck, Bohr, and Schrödinger made the proper applications of this signal to cosmic energy generally, and a psychologist named Jung expressed in better scientific language than Gotama or Hume its application to consciousness.

---

* *Addendum:* As predicted, when the superiority of the "Queen side" was discovered, the event was synchronous with such related *right-hemisphere* phenomena as the use of Oriental perspective in Occidental painting; the Bohr-Schrödinger discoveries mentioned above; the rise of Feminism; rapid evolution from "psychology" to precise neuroscience; creation of synergetic geometry and holistic philosophies of evolution; a *Yin* revolution; etc.

It is further hoped that the 64 squares of the total chess board will eventually transmit the concept of the 64 codons of the genetic code, especially since we have already infiltrated this suggestion into the 64 hexagrams of the *I Ching*. Even if the 8 × 8 structure does not totally communicate the Law of Octaves to them, we have reason to hope that within a kral or two they will at least stumble upon the eightfold nature of the Periodic Table of Chemical Elements.

To represent their present primitive stage of self-awareness, we employ eight pawns. Each pawn represents an ego state, and the primates will easily *identify with* each pawn as they move it. The fact that there are eight pawns, not one, will, we expect, give them some subliminal suggestions about the narrowness of their "one ego" view of themselves.

We have also arranged the metastructure of the game so that the quickest win can be obtained by sacrificing the first pawn moved (if the opponent is gullible enough to succumb to the "grab-at-once" or "attack-at-once" reflex, without using the higher brain circuits). The art of sacrificing pawns skillfully, to win the larger game, will, we hope, insinuate into the Terrans an awareness of the necessity to sacrifice each and any ego state for the maximum functioning efficiency of the brain as a whole. In short, the player who is attached to or identified with any given ego state (pawn) will be defeated by the player who thinks in gestalts, using the whole board, i.e., the whole-brain model.

The other eight pieces, like the eight pawns, hint again at the Law of Octaves, and reiterate once more that the single-ego view of consciousness is false, for each piece represents a different mode of consciousness or a separate brain circuit.

The king's rook, which can move only orthogonally, forward, back, or sideways, represents *the most primitive amphibian circuits of the brain,* having to do with biosurvival fight-or-flight reflexes. The orthogonal symbolism also correlates with the crawling of the newborn infant, when this circuit is being imprinted. The double symbolism is, we submit, neat but not gaudy.

The king's knight, which leaps up from the board to descend in an unexpected place, represents *the mammalian predator who leaps upon the prey.* Since this section of the brain is imprinted in the stage wherein the infant rises up, walks, and begins struggling for power in the pack or family, the up-down symbolism is, we think, neurologically apt.

The king's bishop, which moves on the diagonal, represents *the semantic circuit, which creates Euclidean 3D reality maps* in the primate brain. We put it on a diagonal, instead of at right angles to the orthogonal rook and up-down knight, because 3D chess is beyond the primates at this point.

The king, which stays at home, represents *the fourth circuit: mating and reproduction.*

Thus we have provided a complete model of the circuits of the left brain, standing before the right hand of the "white" player and hinting powerfully of the right-hand/left-brain feedback loop.

The queen side contains a complete model, in turn, of the extraterrestrial circuits waiting to be activated by DNA-RNA signals at the proper evolutionary time.

The queen's rook represents the more intense/less intense modulations of *the neurosomatic circuit.*

The queen's knight, which contains many surprising potentials that chess players will not discover for at least a tnek, represents *the electronic perspectives of the sixth, metaprogramming circuit.* *

The queen's bishop, moving diagonally like the king's bishop, represents *the neurogenetic circuit of DNA evolutionary intelligence,* as contrasted with the narrow egotistic intelligence of the individual primate.

The queen herself, the only piece that can move any distance in any direction, represents *the neuroatomic circuit,* beyond all their concepts of space and time. (She also represents Our Lady of the Stars, but it will take an oroblram before they figure that out.)

---

* *Addendum:* Not until the twentieth century of their calendar did the Terran primates discover that it was stronger to move the queen's knight out before the king's. Male chauvinism blinded them to many of the strengths of the queen's side.

Finally, to illustrate that any mode of consciousness can graduate through HEAD work to the neuroatomic transtime perspective, we have arranged the rules of the game so that *any pawn, by moving upward to the eighth rank* (i.e., through the eight brain circuits), *can become a Queen, i.e., a space-time traveler.*

We confidently believe, Your Vastness, that the chess game will be one of the most successful educational devices we have introduced to the Terran primates.

𝕴𝖙𝖊𝖒

Hey, man, are you using only half your brain?

Phil Gardner

You're pretty hip. We all know that.

You can throw an *I Ching* hexagram and intuit its meaning. You know all about Hedonic Engineering and staying high. You've seen through all the social games.

When it comes to the neurosomatic circuit of the brain, and body wisdom, you're a champ. And everybody knows it.

But what about those mysterious left-hemisphere brain functions? Wouldn't you like to learn the secrets of the West, previously known only to the adepts at the esoteric Princeton Institute for Advanced Studies? Strange arts like the Equation, which predicts things before they happen, or the Syllogism, which allows you to test an argument for internal validity? Or wouldn't you like to know how the mysterious Stereo works, or what keeps planes from falling out of the sky?

Imagine trying to live with one eye, or one lung, or one testicle.

Isn't it equally a handicap to use only half your brain?

Subscribe to *SCIENTIFIC AMERICAN* (not a religious organization)

Conspiracy Digest

Interview 2

Conspiracy Digest: Jefferson was allegedly a dupe. After all, it was John Adams and his Federalists who put a cap on the American Revolution and laced the constitution with defects that have led our current commu-nazi synthesis!

Wilson: I'm more inclined to blame the defects in the constitution on Alexander Hamilton, as Ezra Pound does in his wonderfully provocative *Impact: Essays on Ignorance and the Decline of American Civilization.* But finding somebody to "blame" for history is Newtonian push-pull thinking. I prefer to analyze events as in modern physics, in terms of *relativistic signals creating alternative reality maps for different observers.* For instance, the California welfare system, on which I lived for two years once (gasp, shudder, arrgh!), seems, if looked at in a linear way, to be nothing but a concerted effort to degrade and destroy the poor. When you look into it more closely, you find that nobody planned it that way; it grew out of constant conflict between the liberals, who wanted one type of welfare system, and the conservatives, who wanted another. The result was a gigantic snafu.

The same is true of the constitution, which, as Beard showed (with much more scholarship and objectivity than either Josephson or Pound), grew out of a real class war between Federalist proprietors and Republican small farmers, and ended up satisfying neither of them. I'm not interested in blaming anybody for anything. Most people, as Bucky Fuller says, are too ignorant to be responsible for what they do. I'm interested in getting the hell off the Planet of the Apes and building free libertarian communes in space, where the Free Mind can develop to its full potential, without the communication jamming of the 24 conspiracies on Terra.

CD: Getting back to Aleister Crowley, do you know anything about his alleged affiliations with German Intelligence during World War I? In Crowley's *Confessions* he admits writing for registered German agent George Sylvester Viereck's propaganda newspaper, *International,* while in New York (1914), but claims he was actually a double agent for British Intelligence. Could Crowley's involvement in the Theodore Ruess (German) Ordo Templi Orientis have led to Crowley's having become involved or instrumental in Establishment conspiracies?

Wilson: I don't know for sure, but it would fit my picture of Uncle Aleister if he worked for both British and German Intelligence and also played his own game against both of them. Never underestimate Uncle Al's sense of humor. Crowley's real game, of course, was the Consciousness-Intelligence Revolution, which will eventually raise humanity out of mammalian territorial politics, as we have already outgrown the gills or tails of earlier evolutionary stages.

CD: In your book, *Sex and Drugs: A Journey Beyond Limits,* you advocate Dr. Timothy Leary's principle that drug use should be voluntary and thus, presumably, oppose any sort of drug-controlled 1984-type society. In spite of the sincere motives of drug advocates, is it not possible that they are unconscious tools of the ruling-class conspiracy? Isn't it probable that the Establishment is planning for a drug-controlled culture, à la Ira Levin's novel *This Perfect Day?* Could the Carter administration's "softening" on drugs (advisor Peter Bourne has launched a trial balloon on heroin, marijuana, and cocaine) be part of a tyrannical, forced drug plot?

Wilson: First of all, I object to the term "drug advocates," which is an inaccurate as calling Kinsey a "homosexuality advocate" because he wrote factually and objectively, without inflammatory propaganda, on that subject. Or calling Justice Hugo Black an "obscenity advocate" because he believed people should have the right to decide whether or not they wanted to read a given book. All Leary and I have ever advocated is that the individual, not the government, should decide what experiments (chemical or otherwise) should be conducted within the individual's own nervous system.

Leary's "Two Commandments for the Neurological Age," 1966, were, first, *"Thou shalt not alter the consciousness of thy neighbor without his or her consent,"* and the second, which is like unto this, is *"Thou shalt not prevent thy neighbor from altering his or her own consciousness."* (Dr. Leary has recently added a Third Commandment, 1975, which says, *"Thou shalt make no more commandments.")*

As the first commandment shows, Dr. Leary has always been most urgently aware of the problem you raise. Our article on

"Brainwashing" in *Neuropolitics* explains how mind-programming works and how to outwit it. Dr. Leary's *Exo-Psychology* is a manual on brain change and on how to become self-programming. Any brainwashing system, even those that use the most powerful metaprogramming chemicals like LSD, can be successfully resisted by those who understand the techniques being used. *Programming, imprinting, and conditioning whole populations can only work where there is total secrecy about what is being done.* I say in all seriousness that the more people who understand the mindfucking techniques dramatized in *Illuminatus!* and scientifically analyzed in *Exo-Psychology,* the safer we all are against misuse of those techniques. Meanwhile, keeping Leary's Two 1966 Commandments in print is beneficial in itself, because every reader has to decide to agree with both of them, to deny both of them, or to agree with one and deny the other. Deciding where you stand on that issue is itself a learning experience. *Do you think anybody but yourself has the right to experiment on your nervous system?* That really is the basic philosophical-ethical question posed by the Neurological Revolution. Remember: the nervous system is what pre-scientific primates call the "self" or the "soul." The "self" at the moment depends on which circuit is activated. The "soul" or metaprogrammer decides which circuit or "self" to be at each time-juncture. Do you want to choose your own "self" or do you want your "soul" on ice?

CD: In *Sex and Drugs* you reveal your acquaintance with Dr. Joel Fort. How do you respond to the U.S. Labor Party's charge, in their book *Carter and the Party of International Terrorism,* that Dr. Fort's San Francisco *Project One* was a "brainwashing center" that spawned the Symbionese Liberation Army synthetic zombies for use by the Rockefeller-CIA in "social drama" operations? Purpose: to justify a police state by creating terrorist episodes.

Wilson: Well, since the USLP doesn't offer any documentation or anything that would pass as evidence in a court of law or a meeting of historians, rebutting them is like hunting for something solid in a tapioca pudding. I would merely say that, under the rules of evidence in civilized nations, no jury would convict Dr. Fort on the basis of the kind of allegations made by the USLP; no sane District Attorney or Grand Jury would indict him in the first place; and no sober police department would even call him in for questioning.

USLP says, for instance, that the *Fort Help* office "houses a fully equipped brainwashing and terrorist command center." That is not evidence; evidence requires testimony (preferably by a qualified expert) that the equipment in Fort Help *has been* used for brainwashing, or at least *could be* so used. Without such testimony, a statement of that sort is allegation, or hearsay, and has no evidential value, however inflammatory it is to the imagination of the naive. I could just as well say that *USLP* headquarters "houses all the equipment to make porno movies and rape old ladies." USLP also points out that Fort is "a former collaborator with Dr. Timothy Leary during the 1950s government-sponsored experimentation with LSD." That sentence is (a) guilt by association, a type of argument known to be invalid in the first place, (b) factually untrue, since Dr. Leary didn't do any LSD research, for the government or anybody, during the 1950s, and (c) *irrelevant even if it were true* (which it *isn't*), since literally hundreds of scientists have worked with Dr. Leary on one project or another over the

three decades of Leary's professional career, and that doesn't prove *anything*, except that scientists often work in teams or groups.

USLP also points out that Fort Help has a mental-patient liberation group "similar to the Heidelberg Mental Patients Collective in Germany that became the Bader-Meinhof gang." The fallacy there was pointed out by Aristotle 2,500 years ago (similarity is not identity). I could just as well say USLP has a typewriter "similar to the one on which the Lindberg kidnap notes were written." I feel silly myself even having to point out such elementary logical fallacies. USLP, in general, seems to aim their publications at people of extreme gullibility and no critical faculties at all. (Also, of course, there are mental-patients' liberation groups all over the country, independent of *Fort Help,* and it isn't even clear if, in this particular slander, USLP wants us to believe that only the Fort group is like unto the German group or that all mental-patients' liberation groups are like unto it. And, of course, they offer no documentation that the German group did turn into a "gang.")

USLP also claims to have found one staff member of *Fort Help* who is, they claim (without documentation), also a member of something called Revolutionary Union. Oh, for Christ's sake, when Joe McCarthy sank that low—finding one member of the Welch law firm who had once been a communist and trying to use that to discredit Welch—even Roy Cohn was embarrassed, and McCarthy's most gullible dupes began to wake up.

Of course, the slanders against many others in USLP's *Carter* book are just as logically and legally invalid, nonevidential, and undocumented as the slanders against Dr. Fort.

I would also like to add in this connection

that every major religion, not just the Old Testament, has some version of the commandment against bearing false witness against thy neighbor. When a man's character is slandered, not just he suffers, but his wife, his children, his parents, often his friends. *Those who make a career out of spreading unproven accusations against other humans can only be forgiven if they really are so ignorant and stupid that they don't know the difference between an assertion and an evidential demonstration.* I think it's awfully late to accept that kind of ignorance as an excuse. I think we have a duty to try to know, and to act rationally, responsibly, and decently. In this connection, I recommend Wilhelm Reich's *The Murder of Christ,* especially the chapter on Mocenigo, the guy who turned Girodano Bruno in to the Inquisition. Reich points out that the slanderer and the assassin are similar types, psychologically; being ugly and unattractive personalities themselves, they can only achieve status parasitically, by "stealing" it from the innocent victims they destroy. Mocenigo wouldn't be remembered at all if he hadn't caused the burning of Bruno, and he only gets a footnote for that. The people who have defamed Freud, Reich, Leary, Fort, Sakharov, Oppenheimer, and other great scientists in our time will also only get footnotes. Who the hell would remember Mildred Brady today if she hadn't been the one who incited the FDA to burn Dr. Reich's scientific books in an incinerator?

CD: A major theme in *Illuminatus!* seemed to be that the authoritarian Illuminati seek to achieve immortality (peak experience?) by inflicting death and suffering, while Hagbard Celine's Legion of Dynamic Discord achieved same through sexual orgasm. How do you defend this apparent dichotomy against those who claim (per-

haps like Freud and some conservatives) that sex and sado-masochism are inseparably one? Surely this seems to be the position of the Marquis de Sade in *Philosophy in the Bedroom.* Was Sade an Illuminatus?

Wilson: Jesus, don't confuse the peak experience with the quest for immortality. I agree with Bergson that the search for immortality is a basic human drive (after all, it's the theme of the oldest novel in the world, the *Epic of Gilgamesh*) but, because of ignorance and primitive technology, it has taken many crazy and malevolent forms. In the allegory of *Illuminatus!,* the Illuminati are seeking spiritual immortality through black magick (human sacrifice), Robert Putney Drake is trying to outwit Death by making it into his company cop—his power kick—and Hagbard Celine quite intelligently is seeking immortality through modern science. See Segerberg's *The Immortality Factor,* Tucille's *Here Comes Immortality,* Ettinger's *Man Into Superman,* and Rosenfeld's *Prolongevity* for current trends in life-extension research and eventual immortality. That's the LE (Life Extension) part of he SMI^{2}LE formula. I can't see why any sane human being would settle for less.

As for the peak experience, that can indeed be achieved in varying degrees by sado-masochism, by polyphase orgasm, or by other methods (isolation, fasting, LSD, etc.). But actually "the peak experience" is a loose and inaccurate phrase; there are 12 ascending states of higher consciousness, catalogued by Dr. Leary and myself in our *Game of Life,* and each of them sequentially is a higher peak. As a libertarian I am opposed to anything that involves coercive misuse or abuse of other human beings; so I will not condone sado-masochism except among totally voluntary participants.

I disagree with Freud about sado-masochism. I think Dr. Wilhelm Reich was right, in *Mass Psychology of Fascism*, saying sado-masochism is a secondary drive that arises only when the primary sex drive is repressed or warped. The anthropologist Malinowski, for instance, found no sado-masochism (and no rape) among the sexually free Trobriand Islanders before the Christian missionaries got in.

Making de Sade one of the Inner Five of the original Illuminati in *Illuminatus!* was one of my little jokes. But who knows...??

CD: Was black writer Ishmael Reed's *Mumbo Jumbo* the inspiration for *Illuminatus!?* Could you give us your reaction to *Mumbo Jumbo*?

Wilson: I didn't read *Mumbo Jumbo* until about 3 years after *Illuminatus!* was finished. The same is true of Pynchon's *Gravity's Rainbow*. The astonishing resemblances between those three books are coincidence, or synchronicity, or Higher Intelligence (take your pick). I love everything Ishmael Reed writes, and I once sent him an official Discordian certificate making him a Pope in the Legion of Dynamic Discord. One of the many hidden jokes in *Illuminatus!* (which is only the tip of the iceberg, being part of a much larger artwork called Operation Mindfuck) is that the Legion of Dynamic Discord actually exists, despite its preposterous sound, whereas some of the more plausible parts of the trilogy are deadpan put-ons. As e. e. cummings said to Ezra Pound, "You damned sadist, you're trying to force your readers to *think!*"

CD: Are you familiar with Francis King's *Satan and Swastika* and Ravenscroft's The

Spear of Destiny? Do you think black-magick Crowley-type cults were behind Hitler and Nazism?

Wilson: I'm familiar with most of the literature on Nazi occultism, and puerile stuff it is. The writers all disagree about which occult trade union really controlled Hitler, and every writer tends to blame it on the one occult group he is personally most paranoid about. Crowley's Ordo Templi Orientis was banned by Hitler, and Karl Germer, Crowley's successor as Outer Head of the OTO, spent several years in a concentration camp (where he very intelligently occupied himself with the invocation of the Holy Guardian Angel and came out higher than he went in). My impression is that Hitler was a medium, not a true shaman, and hence subject to obsession and possession by all varieties of insane, weird, destructive influences and entities.

CD: Do you think Hitler was influenced by Crowley's mysterious *Book of the Law*, as claimed by Crowley in *Magick Without Tears?*

Wilson: Crowley didn't claim Hitler was influenced by the *Book of the Law*, just that one of Crowley's German disciples tried to get Hitler interested. If she succeeded, and Adolph actually looked into it, the results were as prophesied in the *Book* itself: "*There is a great danger in me; for who doth not understand these runes shall make a great miss*" (II, 27); and "*The fool readeth this Book of Law, and its comment; & he understandeth it not*" (III, 63).

44

The picture of the captured Viet Cong officer being shot through the head by Brig. Gen. Nguyen Ngoc Loan tripped a kind of emotional trigger in the United States. Rep. Henry Reuss (D-Wis.) protested the killing as "horrible." The chairman of the Joint Chiefs of Staff, Gen. Earle Wheeler, felt required to suggest that Gen. Loan acted more in a flash of rage than in cold blood. Newspapers have had a spate of letters objecting to the picture as too brutal for tender eyes.

There is not much point now in going queasy over a picture of one man shooting another; there is worse to come. There is not much point at this moment in debating the quality of the South Vietnamese leadership or their enthusiasm. They are what we've got and our only option is to bring forth the best effort we can, and hope it is good enough.

President Johnson was right in saying that it is not so much our power as our will and our character that are being tested here, and character starts with a strong stomach.

Chicago Daily News
February 7, 1968

Christian Prayer, 1968

Help us, Prince of Peace, we pray,
To keep strong stomachs as we
    slay,
And, gentle Jesus, give us Will
Not to vomit when we kill.

Though the whole world turn away
Full of anger and dismay,
Let us keep our lunches down
And maintain an iron frown.

Give us Character, dear Lord,
Not to wince when we're
    abhorred,
And save us from the vice of pity
As we napalm hut and city.

Dear God (and dear *Chicago
    News*)
Just as Eichmann killed the Jews,
We must kill again tomorrow:
Empty us of guilt and sorrow.

Simon Moon

45

Science Fiction Review

Interview 1

Science Fiction Review: The theme of "immanentizing the Eschaton" runs throughout *Illuminatus!*, but the phrase is never defined or explained. In the framework of the book, this seems to imply that various secret societies are working to bring about the end of the world. Is that a valid interpretation?

Wilson: The phrase was coined by a Christian historian, Eric Vogelin, and refers to the Gnostic doctrine that people aren't really as hopelessly mired in Original Sin as Christians think. *Eschaton,* from the Greek, means the last thing, and, in Christian theology, this would be Heaven. "Immanentizing the Eschaton" means seeking Heaven within the "immanent" universe, i.e., the only universe we know.

To a thoroughgoing Christian pessimist like Vogelin, anybody who tries to be happy or make others happy is dangerously close to Gnostic heresy. I am all for immanentizing the Eschaton in this sense, next Tuesday if possible. Vogelin detects immanentizing tendencies in humanists, liberals, technologists, optimistic philosophies of evolution like Nietzsche's, communists, anarchists, and most of the post-medieval thought of the Western World, all of which are overtly or covertly aiming at the *verboten* "heaven on the material plane."

In the novel, we make the point that conservatives are also in danger of immanentizing the Eschaton by continuing a cold war that can only result in Hell on the material plane: nuclear incineration.

In one sense, *Illuminatus!* is a *reductio ad absurdum* of all mammalian politics, right or left, by carrying each ideology one logical step further than its exponents care to go. Voltaire used that satirical judo against the Churchmen, and I decided it's time to turn it on the Statesmen. The only intelligent way to discuss politics, as Tim Leary says, is on all fours. It all comes down to territorial brawling.

SFR: I understand the Eschaton theme stems from an anti-Gnostic campaign in the *National Review* some time ago. Could you fill us in on the origins of the term?

Wilson: As I say, it was coined by Vogelin. The anti-Gnostic theme was chronic in conservative circles during the early '60s and even got into a *Time* editorial once. As an ordained priest of the Gnostic Catholic Church, I find this amusing, since it makes most of the educated classes into unknowing disciples of us Gnostics. As Marx said under similar circumstances, "I once shot an elephant in my pajamas. How he got into my pajamas I'll never know."

SFR: How serious are you about the rule of fives and the importance of 23?

Wilson: If *Illuminatus!* doesn't answer that, nothing else will. The documented

46

fact that I have published serious, or at least pedantic, articles on Cabala should add to the mystery. The philosophical point of the book is the reader's own answer to the question, "Is the 5-23 relationship a put-on or an important Cabalistic revelation?" Of course, Cabala itself is a complicated joke, but all profound philosophies turn out to be jokes.

SFR: How serious are you about the Illuminati and conspiracies in general?

Wilson: Being serious is not one of my vices. I will venture, however, that the idea that there are no conspiracies has been popularized by historians working for universities and institutes funded by the principal conspirators of our time: the Rockefeller-Morgan banking interests, the Council on Foreign Relations crowd, the Trilateral Commission. This is not astonishing or depressing. Conspiracy is standard mammalian politics for reasons to be found in ethology and Von Neumann's and Morgenstern's *Theory of Games and Economic Behavior.* Vertebrate competition depends on knowing more than the opposition, monopolizing information along with territory, *hoarding* signals. Entropy, in a word. Science is based on transmitting the signal accurately, accelerating the process of in-

formation transfer. Negentropy. The final war may be between Pavlov's Dog and Schrödinger's Cat.

However, I am profoundly suspicious about all conspiracy theories, including my own, because conspiracy buffs tend to forget the difference between a plausible argument and a real proof. Or between a legal proof, a proof in the behavioral sciences, a proof in physics, a mathematical or logical proof, or a parody of any of the above. My advice to all is Buddha's last words, "Doubt, and find your own light." Or, as Crowley wrote, "I slept with Faith and found her a corpse in the morning. I drank and danced all night with Doubt, and found her a virgin in the morning." Doubt suffereth long, but is kind; doubt covereth a multitude of sins; doubt puffeth not itself up into dogma. For now abideth doubt, hope, and charity, these three: and the greatest of these is doubt. With doubt all things are possible. Every other entity in the universe, including Goddess Herself, may be trying to con you. It's all Show Biz. Did you know that Billy Graham is a Bull Dyke in drag?

Interview with Robert Anton Wilson copyright © 1976 Richard E. Geis, for Science Fiction Review *No. 17, May, 1976.*

Item

TOP SECRET
IMMEDIATE RELEASE TO ALL MEDIA

From: Mordecai the Foul, Illuminati
International, Weishaupt Cabal.
To: Theophobia the Elder, TLETC,
House of Apostles of Eris.

Dear Theo,

No, we are *not* responsible for what is happening to American TV, and I'm surprised that you should imagine we would be involved in such a neurological catastrophe.

Of course, we do control the major networks—nominally, that is. Unfortunately, the mehums we placed in executive positions at the New Bavarian Conspiracy (NBC), the Conservative Bavarian Seers (CBS), and the Ancient Bavarian Conspiracy (ABC) are totally inept and lack all confidence in their own taste and judgment. Since the matter of TV seemed trivial to us, we allowed them to drift and flounder in their own morass.

What these dumb-dumbs did, Theo, was to abdicate all responsibility entirely. They make no decisions at all. They have turned control of the medium over to a mysterious group known as the Nielsen Families.

You may well ask, "Who are the Nielsen Families?"

These are several thousand households selected—*allegedly* at random—by a pollster named Nielsen. What the Nielsen Families look at on the tube supposedly

represents the taste of the whole country (as would be the case, statistically, if they were indeed selected at random).

For a long while, we were deceived along with everybody else. After all, as Henry Louis Mencken once said, "Nobody has ever gone broke by *underestimating* the intelligence of the American people." But then, with the sinister increase in shows like *Laverne and Shirley* and *Tic Tac Dough*, we began to wonder. We conducted our own secret investigation.

What we found, Theo, was that the Nielsen Families were *not* selected at random. Our old antagonist, Mr. Markoff Chaney, had gained access to the Nielsen Corp. headquarters at night, reprogrammed the computer entirely, and selected his own candidates for the Nielsen Families.

Chaney, if you haven't heard of him, is an electronics whiz with a strong grudge against the establishment, based on the facts that (a) he is a genius and (b) he is three feet tall and hence regarded as "cute" by the normal-sized majority.

What Chaney did was to select only the following groups to be part of the Nielsen sample of American taste.

1. Descendants of the famous Juke family, dull-average morons studied in a pioneering genetic survey of the last century. Chaney found every surviving Juke in the

United States, and included them in the Nielsen group.

2. Descendants of the Kallikak family, imbeciles who were the subject of a famous Supreme Court case over fifty years ago.

3. Descendants of the Snopes family of Yoknapatawpha County, Mississippi, a clan renowned for bestiality, idiocy, and greed.

That's all there was to it, Theo. The Nielsen people never discovered how their computer had been snafued. The TV execs have never had the courage to offer anything not immediately pleasing to the Nielsen Families. And thus it has come about that American TV consists only of shows that are comprehensible and amusing to the idiots, morons, and imbeciles of the Juke, Kallikak, and Snopes families.

I know you will find this hard to believe, especially since you have more than once voiced your suspicion that, as you say, "a True Illuminatus is a Master Put-on Artist." I assure you, Markoff Chaney really exists; in fact, there are several novels about his exploits for sale right now.

Also, Theo, if you don't believe this explanation, how do *you* account for the taste of the Nielsen Families?

MORDECAI THE FOUL is High priest of the Head temple of the Bavarian Illumi- nati. *"Since the Illuminati are all atheists,"* he says, *"I don't have many priestly duties to perform—except a Black Mass now and then—so I spend most of my time hanging around Washington and Wall Street, getting to know the Trilateral Commission people and planting evidence, here and there, that we in the Illuminati are still running the world. The gang who really run the world pay me for it, you see, because as long as people blame us for what's going on the real conspirators are safe. Actually, we Illuminatuses gave up politics long ago and now devote ourselves to Cabala and quantum physics. You won't tell Mae Brussell, will you?"* Mordecai is suspected by many of being a shameless Put-On Artist.

THEOPHOBIA THE ELDER is an imaginary being created by Mordecai the Foul. Since he is fairly bright, Theophobia has figured this out and knows he has no real existence aside from the mind of Mordecai. Nonetheless, he still relapses into taking himself seriously on occasion.

49

Ten Good Reasons to Get Out of Bed in the Morning

This is for all you people who lie in bed every morning and wonder if it's going to be worth the trouble to get up. So the job is a drag, your friends let you down, and the price of coffee is outrageous. Listen to me. I have survived two bouts of polio. One of my daughters was gang-raped by three hoods in 1971; another, my youngest, was brutally murdered in 1976. Yet, to quote Faulkner's Nobel Prize address, I still "decline to accept the end of man." I firmly believe that we are entering an age that will make the Renaissance look like a tempest in a teapot, and that each of us can play a role in turning man into superman.

An old Sufi legend: The venerable sage Mullah Nasrudin was once condemned to death for certain witty and satirical sayings that disturbed the local Shah. Nasrudin immediately offered a bargain: "Postpone the execution one year," he implored the Shah, "and I will teach your horse to fly." Intrigued by this, the Shah agreed.

One day thereafter, a friend asked Nasrudin if he really expected to escape death by this maneuver.

"Why not?" answered the divine Mullah. "A lot can happen in a year. There might be a revolution and a new government. There might be a foreign invasion and we'd all be living under a new Shah. Then again, the present Shah might die of natural causes, or somebody in the palace might poison him. As you know, it is traditional for a new Shah to pardon all condemned criminals awaiting execution when he takes the throne. Besides that, during the year my captors will have many opportunities for carelessness and I will always be looking for an opportunity to escape.

"And, finally," Nasrudin concluded, "if the worst comes to the worst, maybe I *can* teach that damned horse to fly!"

Nasrudin was expressing the key element in the Sufi view of the world, which holds that each man and woman is an incarnate part of God, with infinite chances to improve his or her circumstances and likewise to improve the world. "Maybe the damned horse can fly" is a Sufi proverb, indicating that it is always premature to abandon hope.

We live in an age when despair is fashionable, even chic; when human self-contempt has reached heights not known since the Dark Ages; and when it is considered naive to believe that anything good can ever be accomplished. This is partly due to the trauma of the Vietnam war, in which many learned for the first time that Americans can be as beastly as Germans; partly due to the

50

Nixon counterrevolution, in which the optimism and utopianism of the Sixties were clubbed to death; and partly due to the exposure of Nixon and his cronies, which made millions of previously trusting mainstream Americans aware that their highest officials can be liars, thieves, and worse. We have lived through the slaughter of innocence and, like embittered adolescents encountering the harshness of life for the first time, we are afraid to trust again or to entertain hope.

I believe that I have as good reasons as anyone to be depressed. Besides my personal misfortunes, I have been visiting prisons for three years now, and I know the horrors of what our society looks like from the very bottom, from the black holes of isolation cells where men are chained like beasts. Twenty years ago, I worked as an ambulance attendant in Harlem, and I saw what poverty and racism can do at their worst. Nobody needs to teach me anything about the inhumanity of humanity. Yet I still believe that there is, as the Sufis say, a divinity within each person that can be released if love and faith and optimism can be released.

In that spirit I offer the following ten reasons for hope.

One. Consider for a moment the implications of what sociologists call the self-fulfilling prophecy. Simply stated, this means that if you are sure a woman will reject you, you won't make a pass at her. If you believe you can't pass the examination, you will not bother to study. If you think you can't get the job, you won't go for the interview. As a result, the lady will bed down with somebody else, the exam will be passed by those who did study, and the job will go to one of the guys who made an effort to get it.

The outstanding example of the negative self-fulfilling prophecy in our century is Joseph Stalin, who always believed himself surrounded by enemies. His own party, he suspected, was permeated by deviationists who hated him. He steadily increased the size and powers of the secret police, and each chief of the secret police, in turn, was executed as one of the plotters against him. They all signed confessions before they died; Stalin insisted on that. He wanted it in black and white, proof that his suspicions were justified. Eventually, it appears, his closest associates conspired to poison him.

Stalin's paranoia was a self-fulfilling prophecy; so was Bucky Fuller's optimism.

In contrast, there is the case of R. Buckminster Fuller, who stood one day in 1928 on the shore of Lake Michigan contemplating suicide. He was despairing because of his daughter's death by polio and his own lack of financial success as a construction engineer. But, in a moment of Sufi insight, Fuller decided to gamble that the universe had some use for him. Today, he is not only one of the most influential scientists in the world, the inventor of a new system of mathematics and a universally respected philosopher and poet, he is also a multimillionaire. He is one of the most radiantly optimistic men on this planet, as everybody who has ever heard him lecture will appreciate.

Stalin's paranoia was self-fulfilling; Bucky Fuller's gambler's optimism was also self-fulfilling.

Now, let's not confuse self-fulfilling prophecy with the puerilities of positive thinking or other Pollyanna philosophies that ignore reality totally in favor of a cocoon of self-delusion. Bucky Fuller, for instance, has had his share of hard times since his act of faith in 1928. His dymaxion automobile cracked up on a trial run and was never mass-manufactured. His most important scientific ideas were ignored for nearly two decades during which he was dismissed as a brilliant crank. He has experienced the usual human bereavements. Nevertheless, he transcended all such setbacks by believing that he could do something good in this universe.

Two. There is evidence to suggest that our situation is every bit as hopeful as it is desperate. As Alvin Toffler noted in his famous book *Future Shock,* there are more scientists alive and working today than in *all* previous history combined, and this means that we will see more changes in the next two decades than in any 1,000 years of the past. These changes need not be for the worse. If science gave us the atomic bombs that demolished Hiroshima and Nagasaki, science has also, for example, practically abolished smallpox in just ten years. World Health Organization figures are: in 1967, total reported smallpox victims on earth, 2,500,000; in 1976, total smallpox victims, less than 40 (and those were confined to Somalia).

Societies, like individuals, are subject to the self-fulfilling prophecy. If we believe that science will produce nothing but worse Hiroshimas, then that is likely to happen. If we believe that science can conquer every disease, as it has vanquished smallpox, then that is also likely to happen. After all, we put our money and our energy where our beliefs lead us.

Biologist Dr. W. H. Thorpe, of Cam-

1967: total smallpox victims, 2,500,000.
1976: total smallpox victims, 40.

bridge University, speaks for the majority of informed scientists when he says that the breakthroughs of the next generation will "rank in importance as high as, if not higher than, the discovery of fire, of agriculture, the development of printing, and the discovery of the wheel." Our situation is in fact bluntly stated in the title of one of Fuller's books, *Utopia or Oblivion.* What we need to realize is that utopia is just as likely as oblivion. It all depends on where we put our energy, our money, our beliefs, and our efforts.

For instance, Fuller once took the living standard of the top 1 per cent of the US population in 1900 as a base definition of affluence and calculated how many Americans are now affluent by that standard. The answer is over 60 per cent. The trend curve is to reach 100 per cent by around the year 2000. Despite the gloom-and-doom mongers, there is no reason why this cannot happen, although pessimism is certainly one of the factors that might indeed prevent it from happening. The abolition of poverty in the rest of the world could follow soon after, according to Fuller's trend curves.

Three. The actual energy problem of this planet is not nearly so bad as the prophets of apocalypse would have us believe. Using the most sophisticated modern computer-projection techniques, physicist Dr. J. Peter Vajk studied all the relevant technological and economic trends, and reveals in *Techno-*

logical Forecasting and Social Change that we can easily obtain all the electrical energy we will need by the year 2000 simply by using solar power. He urges the construction of the L5 space colonies designed by Professor Gerard O'Neill and his group at Princeton.

O'Neill's space habitats will not take much from the Earth in the way of resources, since 98 per cent of the materials needed can be extracted from the Moon. No new technology is needed for these space cities; we can start building them today with the hardware we already possess. And, according to Dr. Vajk's computer projections, the solar energy these L5 cities and towns can beam back to Earth will meet the energy needs of both the advanced nations and the backward nations, even allowing the most underdeveloped lands to reach parity with the US early in the next century. As many historians have noted, the principal cause of war has always been economic competition for the *limited* resources of this planet. Once we begin tapping the *unlimited* resources of outer space, there is reason to think that pragmatic alternatives to this bloody competition can be found.

Four. None of these future possibilities is reserved for the unborn. There are excellent reasons to believe that all the life-expectancy tables used by insurance companies are already obsolete. You will probably live a lot longer than you expect.

In the very first article that I wrote on life extension (San Francisco *Phoenix*, 1973), I quoted the latest estimate of Dr. Johan Bjorksten, who spoke at the time of extending human lifespan to 140 years. This year, Dr. Bjorksten predicts that humans will soon be able to live 800 years. Paul Segall, of the University of California at Berkeley, who has experimentally stopped the aging

You will probably live a lot longer than you expect.

process in laboratory animals, hopes that his work will extend the human lifespan to 400 or 500 years before 1990. Dr. Robert Phedra puts the number even higher; he says that we can begin aiming to extend human lifespan to 1,000 years.

Look at it this way: life expectancy in Shakespeare's day was about 30 years. (That's why Shakespeare wrote of himself so often as aging and declining in sonnets written when he was only in his early 30s.) In England, 100 years ago, life expectancy was still less than 40 years among members of the working class. It was 60 around the turn of the century in this country. It is now 72. Even if Bjorksten, Segall, Phedra, and the hundreds of other longevity researchers are overly optimistic, even if we can raise lifespan only 50 per cent in this generation, that still means that you will probably live at least 30 years past the projected 72.

In the meantime, the research continues. Within even a 30-year bonus of extra years, the leap into the hundreds of years is likely to occur. For instance, if you are in your 20s now, you expect to die around 2030. Add 30 years to that, and you will live to 2060. How many more years will science be able to give you by then? Even assuming that those researchers currently speaking of life extensions of hundreds of years are doing so too soon, in 2060 an increase of 100 years will be a conservative projection. So you can live on to 2160. And where will the life-extension sciences be by then?

Five. The abovementioned research next opens up the most momentous possibility in the history of evolution on this planet: the chance of real physical immortality. By the gradual increment of life-extension breakthroughs we have been discussing, it is thinkable that some people alive today will never die. We are the first generation in history to have immortality as a scientific, not metaphysical, possibility. Every decade you survive increases the chances that you will live until the crossover point where longevity blends into immortality.

In Osborn Segerberg, Jr.'s *The Immortality Factor,* some recent estimates of that crossover point are quoted. Arthur Clarke, in 1961, set the point *late* in the 21st century. A poll of 82 life-extension researchers in 1964 showed growing optimism and a prediction that chemical control of aging would be achieved by *early* in the 21st century. Another poll in 1969 found a spectrum of predictions ranging from 2017 (the highest estimate) to 1993 (the lowest). As Dr. Timothy Leary points out in *Terra II,* the largest amount of research with the most encouraging results has taken place *since* that poll.

In 1976, F. M. Esfandiary predicted the crossover to longevity would happen by 2000. In 1980, Dr. Alvin Silverstein predicted it by 1990.

Many interested citizens, following the lead of physicist R. C. W. Ettinger, who wrote *The Prospect of Immortality* back in 1964, have formed cryonics societies to freeze their bodies at clinical death, in the belief that future science will be able to revive them and give them a second chance. Although this method of preserving the body is available now only to the affluent, many believe that cryonic preservation of the brain, which costs as little as a few hundred dollars per year, gives an equally good chance of a person's revival — through cloning.

Six. All the possibilities we are discussing here — the abolition of poverty, the economy of abundance for all, the end of territorial competition for limited resources leading to the warfare cycle, the achievement of longevity and eventual immortality — all these are appreciably increased by the appearance of a totally new phenomenon in human life; indeed, a phenomenon so new we hardly have a name for it. Dr. Leary uses the symbol I^2 (intelligence squared) to represent this new evolutionary factor; it stands for intelligence studying intelligence, the nervous system studying the nervous system. Dr. John Lilly refers to it as the self-metaprogrammer, the human brain feeding back self-change directions to the human brain *scientifically.* In simple language, man is graduating from being the conditioned animal in the behaviorist cage to becoming whatever he wills to become.

Part of this mutation will result from drugs similar to, but more specific than, the notorious Sixties psychedelics. Some of the change will come as a result of biofeedback training. Researchers have already taught their subjects how to achieve yogic blissouts in weeks instead of the years of training required by ordinary yoga. Some have learned voluntary control over emotional-physical states of many sorts, including blood pressure and the erection of the penis; others have been able to increase their ESP and other psychic abilities.

Electrical brain stimulation opens other doors to self-metaprogramming. New drugs are predicted that will allow us to foster or terminate emotional states of many kinds. Like the incremental advance from longevity to immortality, this opens a whole new ball game. As Leary points out, "The more conscious and intelligent you become, the more you want to become even more conscious and intelligent." Until now, we

Even such geniuses as Da Vinci, Beethoven, Einstein are partial foreshadowings of what we may become.

have never come close to understanding the self-teaching capabilities of the human brain. It is possible, and not unlikely, that even such geniuses as Da Vinci, Beethoven, or Einstein are only partial foreshadowings of what the turned-on brain can do.

Seven. We are on the edge of abolishing toil and drudgery—work, in the ordinary sense of that word. As Aristotle pointed out, cynically but accurately, 2,500 years ago, "There is only one condition in which we can imagine managers not needing subordinates and masters not needing slaves. This condition would be that each instrument could do its own work, as in a shuttle weaving of itself." Such a totally automated society has been coming closer for nearly three decades now; the inventor of cybernetics, Professor Norbert Wiener, foresaw it as early as 1948.

Fuller, Howard Scott, Dr. L. Wayne Benner, and dozens of other technologists have pointed out that the only reason such total automation does not exist yet is misguided ideology, not lack of hardware. Politicians, for instance, are always promising a cure for unemployment, as if unemployment were a disease instead of the natural condition of any advanced technological society. As Fuller points out, if we count energy in Aristotle's slave units (the amount of work one enslaved human can do in one day), then the average American

owns 300 mechanical slaves in the form of machines servicing her needs.

We do not take the logical and practical next step of automating everything that can be automated only because we are blocked by traditional habits of thought. These habits cannot survive oncoming abundance, oncoming longevity, and oncoming neurological freedom. We go on squandering the most precious resource we have—human brains—by condemning people to pointless jobs that are increasingly unnecessary and that are maintained only by labor unions fearful of lower wages. When we fully accept unemployment as the *cure*, not the disease, we will find that there are dozens of ways, outside the traditional wage system, to distribute abundance equitably: cybernation plus space colonization plus Leary's I^2 will create an abundance that will make poverty as obsolete in 2001 as smallpox is now.

We need to remember that about 97 per cent of all humanity's art, science, culture, and philosophy has come from economically secure aristocracies supported by human slaves. When all humanity becomes an economically secure aristocracy supported by mechanical slaves, Aristotle's imagined utopia will be practical. Immeasurable intelligence will be released to seek goals even beyond immortality, perhaps beyond spacetime as we know it.

Eight. All that we have been discussing is only the tip of the iceberg, the visible part of the possible future. We are actually undergoing a greater philosophical revolution than those associated with Copernicus, Darwin, and Einstein. Our whole world view is literally mutating to a new level of awareness.

Cleve Backster, Marcel Vogel, and dozens of plant researchers claim to be able to communicate with vegetative intelligence.

Dr. Jacques Vallee, cyberneticist, asserts that, in addition to tens of thousands of laypersons who claim contact with extraterrestrials, there are more than 100 trained scientists in the US alone who have had that experience. Dr. Jack Sarfatti, who is one of the 100 and who has come out of the closet about it, says that the entities may be extraterrestrials or time travelers or something for which science has yet no label.

The majority of advanced races in this galaxy may already have immortality.

This revolution can't be defined in ordinary terms, either scientific *or* spiritual. Our whole understanding of science and faith is being radically mutated. Just this year, Dr. Ronald Bracewell, professor of engineering and astronomy at Stanford, and Dr. Frank Drake, astronomer at Cornell, announced their belief that "we'll learn the secret of longevity from space aliens who are trying to communicate with us right now." These are distinguished men who are careful of their reputations. Dr. Drake later wrote in the prestigious *Technology Review* of M.I.T. that he now believes the majority of advanced races in this galaxy *have* immortality.

Nine. The worse our present crises become, the more the pressure increases on us all to find real solutions. We stand at the pivot of human evolution. We now have the technology to blow ourselves up 1,700 times over, thus rendering the planet absolutely sterile, destroying flowers and fish and birds and everything else in a blaze of planetary madness. We also have, or are rapidly developing, the technology for all the once-utopian scenarios discussed here. A world without poverty. Without national rivalries and wars. Without emotional twisting and vast waste of intelligence. A world of immortals who can explore all spacetime and who can contact more advanced immortals.

The more real this paradox becomes to each of us, the greater the pressure to transcend. Every decade is important now: we can choose utopia or oblivion by means of only a few decisions. We cannot evade or escape for much longer. We have to take responsibility and stop laying it all on the other guy. We are being forced to understand John Donne's deathless metaphor: "Never send to know for whom the bell tolls; it tolls for thee."

Ten. If no decisions are unimportant anymore, no individuals are unimportant anymore. Plutonium, the most explosive element known to man, is missing and nobody knows who has it. A jolly group calling itself The National Committee to Overthrow the Government Next Tuesday After Lunch has been anonymously circulating schematic diagrams on how to construct a homemade atomic bomb. Terrorism escalates everywhere, along with nuclear proliferation. One Olympic athlete said recently, "We'll soon be having the games in catacombs, like early Christians." Nobody is safe: remember what happened to the Hearst family. As Leary has been saying for ten years, "We can no longer afford to have anyone on this planet being oppressed, or even thinking he or she is oppressed." Fuller's utopia or oblivion is really the only choice left.

"Captain Crunch" (*aka* John Draper) is the famous phone freak who so long amused himself and his admirers by defrauding the phone company. After his recent trial, he revealed that he has found ways to tap the allegedly invulnerable wires of the FBI, CIA, White House, Pentagon, and the US Army, and even how to activate computers to change bank records or fire missiles to start World War Three. According to the San Jose *Mercury*, for revealing all this to the government and for showing them how to install new fail-safes, Crunch had his sentence cut from four years to three months. But Crunch also says that other electronics experts eventually can get by his fail-safes, maybe by next Tuesday after lunch.

Nobody is unimportant anymore.

There we have it, the final reason to get your ass out of bed: we need you. We need you on our side—the side of hope and action—and we need you now. Every decade is a scientific milestone, which means that every year counts as well, and every month, every week, every day. In-deed, at this point, every act of our lives is either a step toward the achievement of all our visions of glory or a step back toward the stupidity and self-pity that can destroy us. Nobody really needs LSD to see the cosmic importance of every minute.

Any single act of love and hope may be the grain that tips the scale toward survival and, conversely, any single act of cruelty or injustice may be the grain that tips the scale the other way.

As Kurt Vonnegut says, "A great swindle of our time is the assumption that science has made religion obsolete. All science has damaged is the story of Adam and Eve and the story of Jonah and the whale." Vonnegut goes on to say that there is nothing in science that contradicts the works of mercy recommended by Saint Thomas Aquinas, which include: to teach the ignorant, to console the sad, to bear with the oppressive and troublesome, to feed the hungry, to shelter the homeless, to visit prisoners and the sick, and to pray for us all.

If we can see and act on the wisdom of those suggestions, we can greet life with the bravery and joy it deserves.

Dissociation of Ideas, 3

Marxists, and socialists generally, have a fine, piercing, brilliant vision of *all* the defects of the present Monopoly Capitalism.

There is no necessity for conservatives or libertarians to blind themselves to these defects which the Marxist so clearly sees. Such blindness may be popular with conservatives, and even with some libertarians, but there is no *need* for it. It is a habit of stupidity.

The conservatives, and the libertarians, have a fine, piercing, brilliant vision of the defects of totalitarian socialism, and of the diluted pseudo-democratic socialisms that are not quite totalitarian yet.

There is no need for radicals, or even for Marxists, to blind themselves to these defects that the conservative so clearly sees. Again, such blindness may be popular, but there is no *need* for it. Intelligence might be better than conformity to one's group.

Try to think of one or more alternatives to Monopoly Capitalism and State Socialism. While you're trying, endeavor not to concoct a blend of the two. Combining smallpox and chickenpox may not be the only, or the best, alternative to those diseases.

If you can't think of any alternatives, you might browse in some of the books where alternatives are suggested, e.g.: *Progress and Poverty*, by Henry George; *Economic Democracy*, by C. H. Douglas; *The Natural Economic Order*, by Silvio Gesell; *Operating Manual for Spaceship Earth*, by Buckminster Fuller; *Individual Liberty*, by Benjamin Tucker; *The Green Revolution*, by Peter Maurin.

Item

Kathy Green

Daddy, Why Did God Make Us?

"Well, honey, some pretty smart people say that God made us to SMI^{2}LE, use our HEAD, and get RICH.

"SMI^{2}LE means Space Migration + Intelligence Increase + Life Extension. Space enough and smarts enough and time enough for all of us to find and express the best that's in us.

"HEAD means Hedonic Engineering and Development. We've told you about that here and there in this manual.

"RICH means Rising Income through Cybernetic Homeostasis. Totally automated industry is inevitable, sooner or later, how-ever many dinosaurs may try to block it. The cybernetic age means the wage-economy being replaced by a National Dividend economy. Folks like Douglas and Pound and Bucky Fuller have seen that coming since the 1920s. The RICH society is one in which everybody will create their own ideas and artifacts. We'll all be in the Creativity game.

"After we learn to SMI^{2}LE and use our HEAD and get RICH, we'll be wise and strong enough to look for real cosmic challenges. That's why God made us, I reckon."

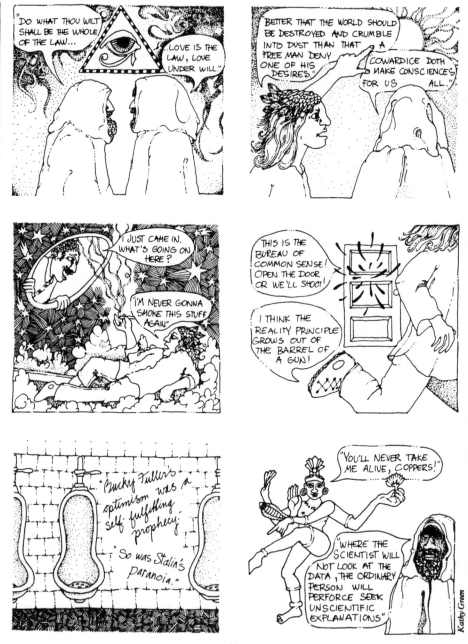

MUSIC DEPT.

Beethoven as Information

Phil Gardner

by Justin Case

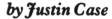

It is no accident that Lenin could not bear to listen to Beethoven (the music made him want to weep and treat people gently, he said); nor that Ludwig's music was banned in Communist China under Mao Tse-Tung; nor that America's leading Marxist theoretician, Herbert Marcuse, has denounced the Ninth Symphony in particular as a Great Lie "invalidated by the culture" which honors it, the culture of Occidental Individualism.

All Marxists, basically, are reactionaries, yearning for the Oriental despotisms of pre-Hellenic times, the neolithic culture that preceded the rise of self-consciousness and egoism. Beethoven as the bard of the recalcitrant individualist is the Homer of music: the "hero," not just of the Third Symphony but of all his works, is really Odysseus, "cunning in stratagems," of whom Zeus said, "Why, with a mind like that he is almost one of us gods!" Such individuals do not arise in pre-Homeric cultures, and are not allowed in Marxist cultures: they are distinctly and distinctively the heirs of Greek truculence.

John Fowles has claimed, in a dramatic context, that *eleutheria* is "the most Greek of all words." *Eleutheria* means freedom, which is what Beethoven's music is all about.

Artistic freedom, of course, is what Beethoven's life was "all about," the constant struggle to push beyond all the limits of music and forge more meaning and more complexity of vision than sound had ever before carried. But the artist, as Joyce has dramatically demonstrated in *Ulysses* and *Finnegans Wake*, is fighting the struggle which every human must fight if we are not to relapse into total robotry: the struggle to see and hear with one's own eyes and ears, not with the circuitry of social conditioning. Beethoven is one man, and struggles, suffers, and triumphs as one, but he speaks for all who are in any degree conscious of their potential individuality.

"Anyone who understands my music will never be unhappy again," Ludwig is alleged to have said. Some biographers doubt the source from which we get this; but it doesn't matter. If he didn't say it, he might as well have; the music certainly says it for him. It is the music of a stubborn individual who is willing to suffer anything, pay any price asked, to achieve greater organic vision than has existed in the world before him.

To be blunt about it, what went on inside Beethoven's head was more important, in the long run, than everything going on outside that head in those years. His music proves it; and that is what the Marxist cannot tolerate about him: that one man should believe himself so important, and what's worse, that he should demonstrate that he *was* so important.

J. W. N. Sullivan, a mathematician and therefore accustomed to precision, defined in one word the deepest response we all have to Ludwig: "reverence." But it is reverence primarily for Ludwig's mind, which could contain so much in such sweet precision, and then for Mind in general, of which he was only one human or super-human transceiver.

Maynard Solomon has described the typical Beethoven structure as combining "irresistible motion and intolerable strain." But that is the formula for all creativity (it could even describe orgasm or childbirth); and it is also the formula of Illumination, of which the Sufis assure us there are three stages, which any listener can hear in the late Beethoven compositions:

1. Lord, use me.
2. Lord, use me but don't break me.
3. Lord, I don't care if you break me.

It is hackneyed, of course, to describe the Fifth as a meditation on Fate; Ludwig started that line of interpretation himself, saying the opening theme represents "Fate knocking at the door." Sullivan was hardly exaggerating when he said the major resolution of the theme is Beethoven "taking Fate

by the throat." Sullivan may or may not be right in his further scanning that Fate chiefly represents Beethoven's growing deafness and the triumphant finale (so bitterly attained) symbolizes Ludwig's realization that he could still compose even when he could no longer hear. It is more likely that the Fifth summarizes everything Beethoven knew about *all* his struggles, including but not limited to the social problems and artistic fears when the deafness was recognized as incurable and progressive; that is why it reflects all my struggles and yours, all the battles we have won and all we have lost, and what we learned in winning and losing.

Nobody but Shakespeare or a damned fool would make an iambic pentameter line out of "never" repeated five times; but Shakespeare does it, and where and when he does it, he produces one of his most powerful tragic effects. And nobody but Beethoven or a damned fool would represent the unity of thesis and antithesis (or the individual Will and implacable Fate) by progressing from the third to the fourth movement without the traditional pause; but Beethoven does it and makes it work. Genius is the capacity to conceive the inconceivable, as Alekhine checkmates with a pawn, while his opponent and every witness was wondering what his knights or queen might be about to do.

There is one moment in literature that is like the end of the Fifth. It is at the climax of *Moby Dick,* when Ahab finally realizes that it was, indeed, "God's will" that the whale should attack its attackers, but that also, in that cosmic context, it must be "God's will" also that he cannot rest until he fights the whale again. "I am the Fates' Lieutenant," Ahab says, and that is what Beethoven had learned in all his struggles against Fate. "I am that which was, and is, and shall be," a quote from an Egyptian prayer, in hieroglyphic and in his own handwriting, was kept under glass on the desk where he composed the late works.

Perhaps some mystics have achieved higher levels of consciousness than Beethoven (perhaps!), but if so, we cannot know of it. Aleister Crowley once astonished me by writing that the artist is greater than the mystic, an odd remark from a man who was only a mediocre artist himself (although a great mystic). Listening to Ludwig, I have come to understand what Crowley meant. The mystic, unless he or she is also an artist, cannot communicate the higher states of awareness achieved by the fully turned-on brain; but the great artist can. Listening to Beethoven, one shares, somewhat, in his expanded perceptions; and the more one listens, the more one shares. Finally, one is able to believe his promise: if one listens to that music enough, one will never again be unhappy.

Ludwig himself? He ended his days as a (relatively) poor, distinctly shabby old man; deaf and lonely; shuffling around Vienna "humming and howling" in an off-key voice as he constructed the music he couldn't hear; furtively sneaking off to brothels because he had accepted, finally, that the Romantic Love he yearned for was not part of his Fate. Some of his neighbors said he was crazy. But what was going on in his head was the creation of the Ninth Symphony, the Missa Solemnis, and the late quartets, the greatest artistic expressions in

> **Beethoven said "Anyone who understands my music will never be unhappy again."**
>
> **The mystic cannot communicate, but the artist can.**

all history of the DNA script of evolution from unicellular dance to the struggles and sufferings of complex organisms to the extraterrestrial perspective of the Cosmic Immortals we are becoming.

JUSTIN CASE is music critic for Confrontation *magazine and won the Congressional Medal of Honor for bravery while serving with the US Army in Vietnam. He prefers his Martinis with vodka instead of gin, hasn't voted since 1972 ("It only encourages them"), and says that anybody who prefers Bach to Beethoven should have their head candled. Mr. Case informs us that he vigorously disapproves of Wagner, Brahms, Democrats, Rock, Soul, Republicans, the Ayatollah Khomeini, and people who put sugar on grapefruit, in approximately that order. In the microscopic list of things he likes (besides Beethoven) are Mozart, Vivaldi, Zelenka, all porn movies featuring Annette Haven, and Bach "when nobody is comparing him to Beethoven."*

Item

Addendum

by Mordecai the Foul, High Priest,
Head Temple, A.I.S.B.

Ever since it was announced in *Illuminatus!* that Ludwig was a member of the Illuminati, we at Weishaupt Cabal have been repeatedly asked whether that particular claim was true or just another of the put-ons with which Shea and Wilson salted that trilogy as a Head Test for the readers.

The fact is that Ludwig Van Beethoven was a member of our Order, as were Mozart and Wagner.*

Since it is widely suspected that the Illuminati are primarily put-on artists, allow me to quote some circumstantial evidence from the latest and most scholarly Beethoven biography, *Beethoven*, by Maynard Solomon (Schirmer Books, New York, 1977).

Pages 26–27: Christian Neefe, Beethoven's first music teacher (after his father

---

* For Mozart, see Will Durant, *Rousseau and Revolution*, page 408. For Wagner, see *Magick, Liber Aleph*, and *Book of Thoth* by Aleister Crowley, in which many clues will be found by the discerning.

and grandfather), was the leader of the Illuminati lodge in Bonn.

Pages 27–28: Neefe was the strongest intellectual influence on Beethoven during Ludwig's adolescence, the most impressionable years of anyone's life.

Page 36: The *Emperor Joseph* cantata, Beethoven's first major work, was directly commissioned by the *Lese-Gesellschaft*, which, as Solomon makes clear elsewhere, and as Robison documents in *Proofs of a Conspiracy*, was the "front" for the Illuminati in Bavaria after we were illegalized in 1785.

Pages 61, 65: Karl Lichnowsky, Beethoven's "foremost patron" in the early Vienna years, was a Freemason. Beethoven had arrived in Vienna with a letter of introduction from the head of the Illuminati lodge in Bonn, Herr Neefe; the Freemasonic lodges in Vienna were all, according to Robison, under Illuminati influence.

These bits of evidence are, as we admitted, circumstantial. The real proof is in the Ninth Symphony, for those who can hear it, and who can understand why the joyous finale is both a political and a mystical statement.

Science Fiction Review

Interview 2

Science Fiction Review: Could you tell us something about the authors and ideas that have influenced you? Are you a long-time science-fiction/fantasy fan? A neopagan or occultist?

Wilson: My style derives directly from Ezra Pound, James Joyce, Raymond Chandler, H. L. Mencken, William S. Burroughs, Benjamin Tucker, and *Elephant Doody Comix*, in approximately that order of importance. Chandler has also influenced my way of telling stories; all my fiction tends to follow the Chandler mythos of the skeptical Knight seeking Truth in a world of false fronts and manipulated deceptions. (Of course, this is also my biography, or that of any shaman.) The writers who have most influenced my philosophy are Aleister Crowley, Timothy Leary, Alfred Korzybski, and Karl R. Popper. Korzybski and Popper (and a few logical positivists) are absolutely necessary for epistemological clarity, especially when you get to the growing edge of science, where the hot debates are going on, and even more if you wander into the occult. Sci-fi and fantasy are my favorite forms of fiction; I think the so-called "naturalists" and "social realists" have committed high treason against humanity by selling their gloomy perspective as the "real" reality. A book that lacks the element of heroism is a crime against the young and impressionable, in my opinion. A book full of anger and self-pity is another crime. Needless to say, as a libertarian I don't mean literally that these are crimes to be punished in court. The only final answer to a bad, sad book is to write a good, funny book. (I love debate and hate censorship. Accuracy of signal and free flow of information define sanity in my epistemology. I should have included Norbert Wiener among the primary influences on my thinking.)

As for neopaganism and the occult: I'm an initiated witch, an ordained minister in four churches (or cults), and have various other "credentials" to impress the gullible. My philosophy remains Transcendental Agnosticism. There are realities and intelligences greater than conditioned normal consciousness recognizes, but it is premature to dogmatize about them at this primitive stage of our evolution. We've hardly begun to crawl off the surface of the cradle-planet.

The most advanced shamanic techniques — such as Tibetan Tantra or Crowley's system in the west — work by alternating faith and skepticism until you get beyond the ordinary limits of both. With such systems, one learns how arbitrary are the reality maps that can be coded into laryngeal grunts by hominids or visualized by a mammalian nervous system. We can't even visualize the size of the local galaxy except in special high states. Most people are trapped in one static reality map imprinted on their neurons when they were naive children, as Dr. Leary keeps reminding us. Alas, most so-called "adepts" or "gurus" are similarly trapped in the first postrapture reality map imprinted after their initial Illumination, as Leary also realizes. The point of systems like Tantra, Crowleyanity, and Leary's Neurologic is to detach from all maps — which gives you the freedom to use any map where it works and drop it where it doesn't work. As Dogen Zenji said, "Time is three eyes and eight elbows."

SFR: Would I be right in saying you probably lean more toward the rightwing form of anarchism than the classical leftist variety?

Wilson: My trajectory is perpendicular to the left-right axis of terrestrial politics. I put some of my deepest idealism into both the Left anarchism of Simon Moon and the Right anarchism of Hagbard Celine in *Illuminatus!*, but I am detached from both on another level.

Politics consists of *demands*, disguised or rationalized by dubious philosophy (ideologies). The disguise is an absurdity and should be removed. Make your demands explicit. My emphasis is on whatever will make extraterrestrial migration possible in this generation. The bureaucratic state, whether American, Russian, or Chinese, has all the clout on this planet for the foreseeable future. The individualist must fulfil his or her genetic predisposition to be a pioneer, and the only way one can do that today is by moving into space faster than anyone else. I think the maverick Seed is included in the DNA scenario to serve that function in each epoch. I'm leaving Earth for the same reason my ancestors left Europe: freedom is found on the expanding, pioneering perimeter, never inside the centralized state. To quote another Zen *koan*, "Where is the Tao?" "Move on!"

SFR: You're involved in an organization called the DNA Society which is interested in biological engineering and immortality, the creation and exploitation of higher forms of consciousness. How serious are you about this? How close are we to achieving this on a broad scale?

Wilson: Let me refer the reader to *The Prospect of Immortality* and *Man into Superman* by Ettinger, *The Biological Time Bomb* by Taylor, *The Immortality Factor* by Segerberg, *Terra II* by Dr. Leary and Wayne Benner, and the writings of John Lilly and Buckminster Fuller.

With that documentation, I assert that the basic longevity breakthrough will occur before 1990. Segall, Bjorksten, or Froimovich, among others, may be very close to it already. The basic principles of reimprinting or metaprogramming the nervous system, as discovered by Leary and Lilly, will be accepted and used in daily practice by around 1985. A neurogenetic quantum jump in life expectancy, intellectual efficiency, and emotional equilibrium (or, as Leary calls it, hedonic engineering) will be revolutionizing human life before the twenty-first century. Some of us will be alive when the Immortality Pill is found.

Interview with Robert Anton Wilson copyright © 1976 Richard E. Geis, for Science Fiction Review *No. 17, May, 1976.*

67

FILM DEPT.

Mammalian Politics
Thackeray via Kubrick

by Justin Case

S tanley Kubrick's new film, *Barry Lyndon,* has received unprecedentedly enthusiastic praise from the Illiterati, that band of vehement and ignorant individuals who write the movie reviews in our daily press. These nosegays of flattery are almost certainly hypocritical, and merely indicate that the Illiterati are afraid to denounce Kubrick at this stage of his career. After all, they mostly rejected *2001* and *Clockwork Orange,* and some of them even downed *Strangelove;* and, despite their carping, all three of those films went on to become box-office dynamite, and got elevated to High Art by the more prestigious critics on the slick quarterlies.

Afraid to denounce *Barry Lyndon,* the Illiterati have instead praised it for all the wrong reasons. It is "beautiful," they say, it is "sumptuous"; it is even "gorgeous"; one would think they were reviewing a three-hour painting by Monet.

Barry Lyndon indeed swarms and bulges with exuberant, almost baroque loveliness, both visually and aurally. (Kubrick has drenched it in even more first-rate music than *Clockwork Orange,* and with more ironic effect.) But the overwhelming tone of the film is not beautiful but tragic, mordant, even moralistic. It is primarily a study in what Dr. Timothy Leary calls "mammalian politics," the most primitive circuits in the human nervous system, concerned with power, status, and emotional game-playing. In ethological language, the subject is territorial behavior among a domesticated primate species.

Barry Lyndon **is a precise neurological dissection of the robot imprints that underlie predatory politics.**

The dominant image of the film is the duel. The opening sequence is a pistol duel, which kills the hero's father and reduces the family to poverty. The dramatic pivot of the opening third is a second pistol duel, which sends Barry into exile. And the climax of the entire film is another pistol duel, one of the most shattering and emotion-churning sequences Kubrick has ever given us.

Other forms of the duel recur emblematically throughout. Card games, usually dishonest, play a repetitious role in the protagonist's rise from Redmond Barry, impoverished exile, to Barry Lyndon, rich nobleman. Duels with the sword become his method of collecting bad gambling debts. To capture the beautiful woman he wants (for her money and status), Barry must first duel psychologically with her inconvenient husband; when the husband is done in and the lady captured, a second emotional duel, with her son, dominates the second half of the film and escalates with slow deadliness to the final pistol duel.

In all of these second-circuit contests (as Leary would call them), the motives are the classic mammalian drives: passion, status, territory (property). Barry is simply another primate, struggling to achieve the one-up position in a typical hominid tribe. Everybody else is struggling also for a one-up position, and each of these higher vertebrates accordingly is simultaneously pushing every other vertebrate one-down. These violent struggles (always inflated by mammalian heroic passions and the mysterious primate sense of "honor") eventually resolve into grubby hustling for money. This is one of Kubrick's prime ironies, but not really either an advance upon or a perversion from mammalian norms. Recent research shows that even chimpanzees can learn to compete for money. Cash is, as ethologists know, symbolic territory.

The naturalistic view of humanity has always been a Kubrick specialty, most notably in the grim parallels between the australopithecines and the astronauts in 2001. Even in Spartacus, burdened by a typically romantic Dalton Trumbo script, Kubrick's Darwinian irony appeared in the cross-cuts between the Roman and slave armies, in which the totems of both the reactionary and the revolutionary forces were suspiciously tribalistic. The Killing, Kubrick's early heist film, portrays cops and crooks as rival predator bands. You can't forget, in watching Kubrick, that few of our ancestors were ladies and gentlemen; the majority of them, indeed, didn't achieve the status of mammalhood, and had the morals and courtesy of Gila monsters.

But Barry Lyndon is as much Thackeray's work as Kubrick's—Thackeray, the least praised and (one suspects) least read of the great Victorians. Nobody is better qualified to resurrect William Makepeace Thackeray than Stanley Kubrick: the two fit each other as snugly as a key in a lock. I once claimed that Joyce invented the "alienation effect" before Brecht; but Thackeray had it even before Joyce. Both Barry Lyndon and Vanity Fair are classic examples of Brechtian-Joycean artistic judo, constantly moving the reader into highly charged emotional-political situations and deftly defusing audience identification at the most crucial points.

Bernard Shaw attempted something of this sort in his Saint Joan, explaining in the preface that he was writing tragedy, not melodrama, and defining the difference elegantly: "Melodrama deals with the conflict of good and evil, tragedy with the conflict of good and good." Not quite; it would be better to define tragedy as the conflict of ambiguity and ambiguity. Here Thackeray and Kubrick excel and mutually reinforce each other. The magnificent, almost Euripidean complexity of the final duel in Barry Lyndon is such that, on the emotional-reflex level, one has been manipulated to sympathize with both parties and with neither of them. The alienation effect of the multiple shocks in that scene—the "turn of the screw," Henry James called it—quite obliterates any emotional identification. One can neither rejoice with the victor nor hate him; nor can one too easily pity the loser. One has been raised above the mammalian politics of the antagonists, cannot take sides any longer, and can only *see* with objective clarity the idiocy of the whole value system that made the tragedy as predictable as a cycle in astronomy.

But one could write a symposium, rather than a single review, about this singularly intelligent film. The handling of the Reverend Runt, for instance, is perfect Thackeray: a caricature worthy of Dickens, but so much more human and complex than any of Dickens' Hypocrites. The parallels with *Oedipus* and *Hamlet* are worth a whole essay in themselves (*Barry Lyndon* is almost *Hamlet* retold from Claudius's point of view). Enough. *Barry Lyndon* is beautiful, yes, but it is much more than that. It is a philosophical *Strangelove*: a precise neurological and ethological dissection of the robot imprints that underlie war and predatory politics.

JUSTIN CASE is film critic for Confrontation *magazine and author of the highly praised history of cinema,* From Caligari to Vlad. *He has a Ph.D. from Yale and a D.D. from the US Army. Dr. Case insists that, although he has written a book, he has never read one, since literature is obsolete. "Only the electronic media are worthy of serious consideration as synergetic cultural signals in the emerging nonlinear postindustrial omniinterfaced global village," he told our interviewer, adding acidly that "the printing press is going the way of the brontosaurus, the dodo, the eohippus and the Vatican: from archaism, to quaintness, to Camp, to extinction." He is usually quite stoned.*

70

𝔍tem

The Eight Basic Winner Scripts

I. The biosurvival winner:

"I will live forever, or die trying."

II. The emotional-territorial winner:

"I am free; you are free; we can have our separate trips or we can have the same trip."

III. The semantic winner:

"I am learning more about everything, including how to learn more."

IV. The sociosexual winner:

"Love, and do what thou wilt." (Anon. of Ibid)

V. The neurosomatic winner:

"How I feel depends on my neurological knowhow."

VI. The metaprogramming winner:

"I make my own coincidences, synchronicities, luck, and Destiny."

VII. The neurogenetic winner:

"Future evolution depends on my decisions now."

VIII. The neuroatomic winner:

"In the province of the mind, what is believed true is true, or becomes true within limits to be learned by experience and experiment." (Dr. John Lilly)

An Incident on Cumberland Avenue

"Blood for blood...."
T. S. Eliot, *Murder in the Cathedral*

On the morning of February 1, 1965, the temperature in Knoxville, Tennessee, fell to 15°, and a mean dose of sleet, rain, and wind began to whip the city. Southerners hate this kind of weather more than Northerners, because they are less accustomed to it. They grumble more than Northerners; they curse more; their tempers grow shorter. When the sleet began to turn to snow around noon, and the weather bureau predicted a six-inch fall, the county schools closed for the day, and the city schools followed suit shortly, sending their pupils home at 1:30. As stalled cars began jamming the roads, everybody resigned themselves to a miserable day.

Records show that the Knoxville police received 117 phone calls requesting assistance during the afternoon and evening: 50 of the calls concerned traffic problems of varying degrees of severity, one of which was a seven-car collision on Kensington Pike; 67 of the phone calls were complaints by motorists who had been pelted by snowballs by University of Tennessee students on Cumberland Avenue, a four-lane throughway which passes in the middle of the campus and joins US Highway 11.

Cumberland Avenue has a difficult hill in its 1700 block adjacent to the university, and a special patrolman was sent to handle

traffic problems there, but the city police took no action about the student snowballing, assuming that the university's private police could handle that, as they had in the past.

Subsequent investigations revealed that the campus police broke up the snowballing at 3:45 that afternoon, but that it had resumed around 4 p.m. The campus police never returned to the scene, being too busy helping faculty members navigate the hills of the campus, many of them in cars which were, Southern fashion, unequipped with snow chains. The Knoxville policeman was on the other side of the hill from the snowballing.

French Harris has been Knoxville's Chief of Police for five years and was a detective for 19 years before that. Many people now want to blame him for what happened that day on Cumberland Avenue, but he has been a cop too long to be overly sensitive to criticism. A burly 50, he started as a motorcycle officer, attended the FBI National Police Academy, and worked for three years with the US Narcotics Bureau. He is popular in Knoxville and popular at the university also. Students know that he will not insist on collecting the towaway fee on an illegally parked car if the driver's hard-luck story is convincing to him. They gripe about the severity of his enforcement of the laws against serving liquor to minors, but about nothing else.

Chief Harris has stood trial for murder twice. Each time he shot an escaping suspect; each time he was acquitted and returned to the force. He is known for his compassion and for his attempt to be fair within the limits of the law.

"I sat on the defendant's side of the courtroom twice," he has said. "I know what it feels like over there."

He took morphine once before going to work with the Narcotics Bureau.

"I wanted to find out what an addict is looking for," he explains. "It's not enough to arrest a man. I want to understand him. Maybe, then, I can help him. And maybe I won't have to arrest him again."

French Harris attended a seminar on civil rights at New York University two years ago, to find out what *that* is all about. He is a man who wants to understand, and to be fair.

At 3:30 that afternoon a man named Roland Lawson drove through the blizzard and the student snowball gauntlet on Cumberland Avenue. Lawson, 58, was a welder at Fulton Sylphon Company in Knoxville and had left work early to have snow chains put on his car.

Roland Lawson had high blood pressure and had been warned by his doctor that undue excitement or strain might bring on a heart attack. The students on Cumberland Avenue pelted his car with snowballs as thoroughly as they pelted all the other cars passing.

Lawson drove half a block further, after passing this gauntlet, and slumped unconscious behind his wheel. The car drove off the road into a telephone pole and came to a stop. Pedestrians called an ambulance and, a few minutes before 4 p.m., Roland Lawson was declared dead of a heart attack at University Hospital.

Nobody at the hospital knew about the

snowball gauntlet Lawson had passed, and French Harris did not hear about this incident for several hours. Nor did he hear that the widow of Roland Lawson had to drive through Cumberland Avenue on her way to the hospital and that her car was also plastered with snowballs by the students, severely angering and frightening her.

And French Harris did not learn, until too late, that when Mrs. Lawson saw her husband's body at the hospital and learned where his heart attack had occurred, she immediately pronounced the theory which was to be carried all over the country by the press on the following day: Roland Lawson's heart attack had been caused by the student snowballing.

Chief Harris did not know this theory at 4:30 p.m., when Mrs. Lawson pronounced it. If he had heard it at the time, he might have acted sooner. If he had, Knoxville would not have found itself with two more corpses to explain.

"Who is the slayer, who the slain? Speak. . . ."

Sophocles, *Oedipus Rex*

At 9 a.m. that morning, Frank Wasserman was awakening his roommate, Marland Goodman, at New Melrose Hall, one of the most modern buildings in the University of Tennessee. Both boys were 18 and Northerners—Wasserman from Massapequa, Long Island, and Goodman from Swamscott, a fashionable suburb of Boston—and they had been close friends ever since the Snipe Hunt.

The Snipe Hunt is an old tradition at the university. The students are mostly natives of Tennessee, but about 10 per cent of them come from out-of-state and from 85 foreign countries. When each new freshman class arrives, these outlanders hear about the wonderful Snipe Hunt.

The snipe is the most delicious bird of all, they are told, even better than the pheasant, and the woods outside of Knoxville are full of them. When the night of the snipe hunt arrives, most of the outlanders are eager to join. The natives lead them out into the woods and then simply lose them there.

There is no such bird as the snipe. Marty Goodman and Frank Wasserman had been among a group of Northerners who went on a snipe hunt in September, 1964, and, lost in the dark in an unfamiliar woods 1,000 miles from home at 3 o'clock in the morning, their status as Northern aliens had drawn them together.

They had learned something about courage and humor and loneliness and each other. We think of the snipe hunt, or the biscuit-gun which Air Force recruits are sometimes sent to look for, or the can of striped paint which apprentices in the building trades are asked to fetch, as mere pranks, but anthropologists call these rites "ordeals of initiation" and say that they provide a catharsis of shame and anxiety necessary to mark a transition from one stage of life to another. The Snipe Hunt meant something of this sort to Wasserman and Goodman.

Of the two boys, Marty Goodman was somewhat better known on the campus. His collection of folk records and folk sheet-music was large, and he was an enthusiastic folk guitarist. He would sooner talk about folk music than about any of his college subjects.

This morning, however, he was not talking about folk music, but about his girlfriend, Judy Goldberg, back in Boston, and complaining about how much he missed her. Frank Wasserman remembered that afterwards.

Marty Goodman also mentioned his mid-term paper for English 112. He had really sweated over this one, and hoped to get an A. He had received two C's and a B-minus on his previous papers in that class. Today at 3 o'clock he would get back his midterm paper and find out if he had achieved the A he aimed for. Frank Wasserman remembered that later, also.

At 2:15 that afternoon, Julian Harris was in his office at the university. A gangling, Lincolnesque 50, Mr. Harris is director of Public Relations for the university. It's the kind of job that keeps you awake nights. Like every other college town, Knoxville seethes with hostility toward the students and regards them as overeducated juvenile delinquents.

Knoxville, also, is the South: When you enter town on Route 11 you pass a sign saying SAVE THE REPUBLIC—IMPEACH EARL WARREN! and the John Birch Society meets in the Hotel Farragut in midtown, and you occasionally see a car still wearing a sign, bitter in defeat, saying "AuH$_2$O—64."

In such an ambience, any university must be viewed with suspicion. When Chief Harris noted that the sleet was turning to snow, he thought at once of the student volunteers who help stalled motorists on Cumberland Avenue during every snowstorm. He hoped that the students would be at that job today; it would be good for the university's image.

By 2:30 the weather was so bad that Dean of Students Charles Lewis, in his office in the administration building, told his secretary to take the rest of the day off. Dean Lewis, a sandy-haired man of 46 addicted to dapper bow-ties, remained in his office for a conference, scheduled for 4 o'clock, with four student leaders—a conference concerning the students' objections to the university's new service fees.

74

He intended to give them great leeway in stating their resentment, listen sympathetically as long as they cared to harangue him, and not reduce the fees a penny. It would be a grueling session.

Looking out his window, Dean Lewis noticed some students engaged in a harmless snowball fight. Smiling, he remembered the smaller snow of a week earlier and his own surrender to temptation crossing the yard in the morning. It is a good feeling, even when you are 46, to pick up a handful of snow, pack it tight and hard, and hurl it at a tree. And, when you are 46, it is good to hit the tree. Dean Lewis was glad, however, that none of the students had observed his outburst.

The students seen by Dean Lewis were not the only ones on the campus who were beginning to succumb to the insidious temptation of the snow. Down on West Cumberland two teams had formed on opposite sides of the Avenue and were bombarding each other over the tops of the passing cars.

Some, more venturesome, were beginning to pelt the cars also. This is a favorite juvenile sport and most of us have had our cars pelted this way once or twice every winter. Some of us are even willing to remember having done some of the pelting when we were young.

Soon over 200 students had joined in the fun. None of them noticed the effect of their snowballing on Roland Lawson.

Further up Cumberland Avenue, on the other side of the hill, students were helping stalled cars get started again. Julian Harris, the PR man, driving his secretary home, noticed them, and felt a sigh of relief at the good image they were creating for the university. He did not know about the image being created on the other side of the hill.

The Knoxville police, however, were already getting an earful of that image.

J. M. Lobetti, President of the White Star Bus Lines, called the police to report that students on West Cumberland had broken 12 windows in a stalled bus at 3 p.m., forced open the door and bombarded the driver, Robert Holder, in the face.

An anonymous cab driver complained of seeing a woman dragged out of her car and pulled by the heels through the snow. "Her pants must've gotten full of snow," he said. "It was awful."

John Rinehart complained that his car had received a broken window, snow was poured in "all over the front seat," and that students had "manhandled" him when he opposed them.

And — in another part of town — university track students snowballed a Negro driver and he went off the road into a ditch. This last case was quickly smoothed over, however. Track coach Frank Rowe was on the scene and he forced students to contribute $50 for repairs of the vehicle and apologize to the driver.

As the mean, cold snow continued to fall, the student mob on Cumberland Avenue increased to more than 400. The air was resounding with skids, stalled motors groaning, drivers cursing, and the hilarious shrieking and laughing of the students.

Patrolman Davis Gaddis, a block away over the hill, was continually approached by motorists with complaints about the gauntlet they had run. He told them, quite correctly, that he could not leave his post, and instructed them to phone police headquarters.

Once or twice, students ranging this far east pelted Patrolman Gaddis himself, an act perhaps profoundly symbolic.

None of the students were "thinking," of course; they were just having fun. But the fun, more and more, was taking on a ritual character, a character of assault upon every manifestation of adult authority. It was inevitable that a policeman, also, would become a target. A policeman represents the most monolithic form of authority: the State.

"For the brothers who had joined forces to kill the father had each been animated by the wish to become like the father and had given expression to this wish by incorporating parts of the substitute for him in the totem feast. . . ."
Sigmund Freud, *Totem and Taboo*

Frank Wasserman, the freshman from Massapequa, was studying in his room at 4 o'clock when Marty Goodman burst in, announcing that several snowball fights were in progress all over the campus and he wanted to get in on the action.

Marty had just had a serious disappointment. Trudging almost a mile across campus to Science Hall for his English 112 class, he had found a notice that class was canceled for that day. His teacher, Mrs. Nancy Fisher, a resident of Oakland, Tenn., had bogged down in the snow and turned back home. Marty would have to wait until Wednesday to learn whether or not he had gotten the A he aimed for on his midterm paper.

Frank loaned Marty a scarf, but declined to join him in the snow carnival. "I want to study for a while more," he said. "I'll be out later."

Frank Wasserman was never able to remember what he studied that afternoon. A little after 6, he gave up for the day and went out to look for action. He found some of it, immediately, at the door of Melrose Hall, where a gang of seven pelted him with an avalanche of snowballs.

Unable to hold his own against these superior numbers, Frank ran, looking for friends. After getting around the corner, he slowed to a walk. Then, suddenly, a student he didn't know ran up to him and said, "You better get back to Melrose Hall. They'll be looking for you. Your roommate's dead."

"I laughed," Frank Wasserman said later. "I was sure it was a joke. They wanted to get me back to the Hall to make a target out of me again. I was sure of it. I said, 'Come on, you're putting me on, fellow.' "

The other student was pale and sober. "It's true," he said glumly. "Marty's dead. He just got shot on Cumberland Avenue."

Frank Wasserman suddenly felt a chill of certainty, and heard himself saying, "Really? Really?" But the other's face had already told him.

Are you washed in the blood of the Lamb?
Are you marked with the mark of the beast?
Come down Daniel to the Lion's den
Come down Daniel and join in the feast . . .
T. S. Eliot, *Murder in the Cathedral*

Cumberland Avenue, when Marty Goodman arrived there shortly after four, was midway between a carnival and a nightmare. Buses, cars, and trucks were stalling, and somewhere between 400 and 500 students were raining snowballs on the entire scene, while the wind whipped and howled and snow continued to fall.

In one of the stalled trucks, William Douglas Willett, Jr., of Greenville, Tenn., fretted and fumed. He was lost. Trying to save time in the heavy snow, Willett had taken a new route through Knoxville and now he was on a street he didn't recognize and snowballs were going *thump, thump, thump* in unending hammer blows on his windshield and he was afraid the windshield might break at any minute, and then, suddenly, the cab door was torn open and a dozen grinning faces appeared looking in at him.

He opened his mouth, angry and frightened, to warn them not to go too far, but before he could say anything they began to dump pounds of snow all over him and his seat and he was hit in the face repeatedly and he reached in his glove compartment and took out the pistol provided by his company.

The students saw the gun and Willett made a threat—nobody ever remembered his exact words—and somebody (Willett later said he thought it was Marty Goodman) threw snow in his face and he got out on the running board and somebody else threw snow in his face and then he fired the gun, twice only.

For one moment, nobody moved.

The echo of the shots hung in the air and all the laughing and shouting stopped and every student held his breath to see if he was hit anywhere and then Marty Goodman crumbled and fell hard like a tree and lay still in the snow with a red stain spreading in the snow around him. The other shot had gone completely wild, but this one hit Marty Goodman in the right eye, crashed through his brain, and exited below the left ear.

With a shriek the students charged Willett. According to some witnesses, as many as 20 students landed in one pile on the truckdriver, dragging him to the ground, kicking him, hitting him, screaming. A girl student screamed, "Don't kill him—he didn't know what he was doing!"

Willett was finally released and allowed to return to his cab, and the police were called at 5:39, one hour and nine minutes after Mrs. Lawson had made her charge, to the hospital staff, that the students had killed her husband.

Marty Goodman's body was carried into Evan's Sundries, a drugstore half a block away. He was breathing. A student named Ken Elrod, 18, from Nashville, gave mouth-to-mouth resuscitation. When the ambulance arrived and Marty Goodman was lifted for the second time, his pulse stopped. Ken Elrod rode in the ambulance to the hospital, but he was not surprised when the doctor in the emergency room, at 6:04 p.m. pronounced Marland Joseph Goodman, 18, a boy who liked folk music, dead on arrival.

"According to the law of retaliation which is deeply rooted in human feeling, a murder can be atoned only by the sacrifice of another life; the self-sacrifice points to blood guilt. And if the sacrifice of the son brings about reconciliation with god, the father, then the crime which must be expiated can only have been the murder of the father...."

Sigmund Freud, *Totem and Taboo*

The snowballing continued, with greater frenzy. The first two policemen on the scene, Detectives Robert Chadwell and Gene Huskey, were snowballed while helping to lift Goodman's body into the ambulance.

Chadwell sounded off to the first reporter he saw. "They have no respect for an officer," he said, "or for anyone else. They don't act like students. They act like a bunch of idiots. One of the snowballs hit me in the back of the head, and it hurt for 30 minutes or longer."

William Douglas Willett was taken to police headquarters and questioned by Inspector Fred Scruggs. Willett was "crying like a baby," Scruggs said later, and kept repeating, "I didn't mean to do it, I didn't mean to do it."

Scruggs learned that Willett was employed by Bird and Cutshaw Produce Company of Greenville, Tenn., and had been driving a load of fresh-dressed poultry to Cincinnati, Ohio. Examination showed that Willett had been bruised on the left temple, nose, and mouth by snowballs, and that his left eye was swollen.

Back at the university, the snowballing was still going on. John F. Roth, a welding truck driver, called police to complain that students on Cumberland Avenue snowballed his truck, jerked open the door, and covered the front seat with snow "with me in it."

Dean of Students Charles Lewis had finished his conference with the student leaders about fees and was about to leave when word of the Goodman shooting reached him. He went at once to the Student Center, where there were more telephones than in any other campus building, and began trying to handle the situation.

Dean Lewis, first of all, was concerned to authenticate the identification of the dead boy. Five years earlier, while he was Dean at the University of North Dakota, a misidentification had been made of a student killed in an auto accident—it turned out later that the student had exchanged wallets with another student for some inexplicable student joke—and the wrong parents were notified that their son was dead.

Dean Lewis, therefore, began a search for someone who could positively identify the body as Marland Joseph Goodman.

Phones in the Student Center rang continually and nobody was quite sure that Willett's second shot hadn't hit another student. It was chaos. Julian Harris, the PR man, could not get back to the university in the storm, but Dean Lewis directed all reporters to Harris' home phone number.

A search of the Records Department revealed that Marland Goodman had an uncle, Prof. Fred Blumberg, on the faculty of the English Department. Dean Lewis contacted Prof. Blumberg and told him, gently, that his nephew might be the boy who was shot. Prof. Blumberg agreed to go with Dean Lewis to the hospital to identify the body.

The drive through the increasingly furious snowstorm was painfully slow, and both men were too emotion-torn to speak much. At the hospital, the identification was brief.

"Yes, that's Marty," Prof. Blumberg said, when the body was shown.

"I remember that moment every day," Dean Lewis said a month later, "and I think I always will, as long as I live."

The sheet was drawn back over the dead boy's face, and the two men walked silently out of the hospital and back to their car to begin again the painful five-mile-an-hour drive through the still-falling snow.

It was 8:30, and back at the university the snowballing was finally ending, but the incident was far from over.

Frank Wasserman returned late that night to the room he and Marty had shared. He looked at Marty's guitar, Marty's books, Marty's sheet music, Marty's records, and started to get undressed for bed. He found that he couldn't sleep in that room.

You read about hundreds, thousands of corpses in the Congo or Vietnam or West Berlin and it means nothing; a boy shares your room for a few months and then suddenly he's not there and it means something more than you can ever speak.

Frank Wasserman put his clothes back on and got out of that room, fast. He stayed in the room of another freshman, Jack Topchick, of Passaic, N.J., that night.

At the same time, approximately, a man named Walter Lee Yow was checking into

78

the Salvation Army shelter in Knoxville. His head was bothering him, and he complained about being hit, while driving a truck down Cumberland Avenue, behind the ear, by a particularly hard snowball with ice in it. Neither the police nor the university were to hear about Mr. Yow until the following day.

February 2nd began as sheer hell for Dean Lewis and Julian Harris. Local reporters, hearing about Lawson's heart attack, grew increasingly hostile in their questioning of university officials.

"I could feel an ulcer starting as soon as I heard about Lawson," Harris said later, "and each reporter made it grow a few millimeters."

It would have grown even faster if Harris had known that Walter Lee Yow awoke that morning, in the Salvation Army shelter, with his head hurting even more, and called the police to volunteer to testify for Willett. "He shot in self-defense," Yow said. "Those students were completely out of hand." Yow agreed to come down to headquarters to make a statement, but said he wanted to see a doctor first.

Dr. Henry Christenberry was the doctor to whom Yow went. A genial 53, he is a native of Knoxville, although he studied at the NYU-Bellevue medical school. Examining the wound behind Yow's ear, Dr. Christenberry decided that it might be serious. Yow suddenly stood up and began walking about agitatedly, complaining of the pain, and then, very slowly, sank to the floor in a coma.

"Ken, come in here!" Dr. Christenberry shouted. His brother, Dr. Kenneth Christenberry, 49, rushed in from the adjoining office. The two doctors worked over Yow's body for half an hour, administering oxygen and adrenalin and then, desperately, massaging his heart. It was no use. At 4:30,

they pronounced him dead "of multiple concussions and brain damage."

The University of Tennessee now had three corpses to explain.

And now that the fury of the students was exhausted, the fury of the townspeople began.

"Passion, I see, is catching. . . ."

Shakespeare, *Julius Caesar*

The Knoxville *News-Sentinel* editorialized that night: "Yesterday's terrifying demonstration by temporary maniacs must never happen again." The people of Knoxville were even more emphatic, and their letters poured into the papers.

Sam T. Hodges of 712 Boggs Avenue wrote:

"The only surprising thing about the shooting of a student in the customary snow riot of educated hoodlums on W. Cumberland was that it took so long to happen.

"The conduct of these mobs is evidence of the vast difference between education and intelligence. . . . The conduct of many of those students is nothing short of heathen idiocy. They show a complete lack of normal human sympathy for persons already in serious trouble."

Manning B. Kirby, Jr., of 8021 Hayden Drive wrote:

"I have no hope that the students involved in the snowballing who read this will be in any way moved by it. I know they are rude and ruthless, completely selfish and vicious. . . . I am completely fed up with the homes that instill such selfishness in them. I am fed up with the university officials who cannot at least provide safe conduct through the campus."

Mrs. Maie Roberts of 2441 Woodbine Avenue wrote:

"Trying to bring a huge truck safely over snow and ice through a blinding snowstorm is cause enough for distress without having a bunch of wild men, operating under the name of students, attack you for the thrill of seeing your distress."

Mrs. W. G. House of Louden, Tenn., wrote:

"It seems that Webster didn't provide a word to define the disgust, nausea, and heartaches that describe the incredible acts of the students at the University of Tennessee. Not only the students are to blame, but what about the staff in charge? . . . One cannot possibly believe that the heathen manner of these students continued while the ambulance attendants were trying to place a dying student in an ambulance. This is proof that they had no love or respect even for a fellow college mate."

Mrs. J. L. Hans of Rockwood, Tenn., wrote:

"I think the crowd of boys who went into the snowballing incident should feel that they have the blood of three people on their hands. Instead of the truck driver being charged and under bond, they are the ones who should be charged.

"The truck driver was only doing what anyone would have done under the circumstances. He was only defending himself."

B. J. Pritchard of 5613 Scenic Hills Road wrote:

"The truck driver will have to pay for the rest of his life with grief, if not in prison, and from his appearance he's the kind that will. Had it not been for this, he would probably have worked hard the rest of his life and harmed no one. He wouldn't have been a doctor or lawyer like so many of the students, but he'd have been a good man, and that's what counts, so they say.

"He'll be tried and probably convicted of murder or something. But what about those who caused the whole thing? They're the guilty ones. Three deaths they caused and not enough humanity about them to cease their inhuman activities after they saw what they had done."

And a student named John S. Moak replied in kind, much to the distress of the university officials:

"I can guarantee, although not personally, that if the courts take your prejudiced view concerning the truck driver that this campus may literally erupt!

"One of my reasons, in fact the main reason, I write this letter is that perhaps I feel that my life is quite cheap if a man can kill 'one of my kind' and get off scot-free."

Dean Lewis, sensitive to the town's emotions, warned students not to write any more such inflammatory letters, but angry correspondence from townspeople continued to pour into the *News-Sentinel* for two weeks.

On Wednesday, English 112 met without Marty Goodman. Mrs. Nancy Fisher, the teacher, found that she couldn't remember what young Goodman had looked like; he hadn't particularly distinguished himself in that class. Returning the midterm papers, she found Goodman's and saw that she had given him the A he had hoped for.

Meanwhile, a committee was started in Greenville, by Willett's employer, Cutshaw, and $100,000 was raised for Willett's defense. Knoxville Police Chief French Harris learned that Willett, a farm boy, was very popular in Greenville, and that his reputation with employers and townspeople was excellent.

"I can understand how that farm boy felt with all those kids throwing snow and ice in his face," Chief Harris reflected to an inquirer. "I can understand the kids, too," he added. "They were just having fun. It's terrible, terrible for everybody."

But Chief Harris was already ordering a skeptical reevaluation of the Walter Lee Yow death. It seemed unlikely, Harris felt, that a truck driver, such as Yow claimed to be, would be staying at a Salvation Army shelter.

A check of trucking lines that pass through Knoxville failed to reveal any Walter Lee Yow among the employees.

Harris then ordered a check to determine if Yow had entered Knoxville by any other means. A bus driver was finally located who positively identified Yow as a man who had ridden into Knoxville on his bus on February 1st at 2 p.m. The bus had not passed anywhere near Cumberland Avenue.

Where, then, had Yow received his injury? Why had he lied about it? Where did he come from, and what were his motives? Chief Harris has learned a few things, but the major mystery remains.

Walter Lee Yow was a "freight handler"—he wandered about the country taking temporary jobs loading and unloading trucks. Evidently, he regarded his job

as less dignified than a driver's job and was in the habit of calling himself a driver. He had hitched a free ride on the bus by pretending to be a driver whose truck had broken down in the snow. No such truck was ever found. Had he perhaps wandered out to Cumberland Avenue and been struck by a student snowball? Chief Harris had doubts about it: The bus driver recalls that Yow complained about his head pain when he picked him up outside Knoxville over an hour *before* the snowballing began.

The mystery of Walter Lee Yow may never be solved.

"Maybe he just wanted to get his name in the papers," Chief Harris says. "Maybe he hoped to get the university to pay for his head injury, wherever he got it. Or maybe the injury affected his brain and he really didn't know what happened to him."

Chief Harris shrugged.

"I try to understand everything that comes in this door, but there's a lot about the human mind I'll never understand. Violence always brings out some people who get mixed up in it for reasons you never understand, and you wonder if they understand it themselves."

"Tell me about the rabbits, George. . . ."
John Steinbeck, *Of Mice and Men*

Perhaps we can hazard a guess at Walter Lee Yow's motives. The people who wrote indignant letters to the Knoxville *News-Sentinel* provide a clue as to what drew Yow into the maelstrom of death on Cumberland Avenue. Like them, he saw a great big beautiful orgy of violence, and wanted to *involve* himself, to impose his own meaning upon it.

His head injury gave him his entrance.

Others had to be satisfied with vicariously pulling the trigger for Willett and

81

defending themselves under the guise of defending him, or, like student Moak, threatening riot if Willett's corpse were not added to the previous corpses. In one way or another, every man sees his own image in what happened on Cumberland Avenue.

A few things have been learned about Yow. He was a bachelor, 55, and came from Aubermarle, North Carolina. Natives of Aubermarle say that he was "nice to children" and always gave lots of candy away to the children in his neighborhood when he visited home. But nobody knows where he got his head injury, and nobody knows, for sure, why he lied about it.

The police were still investigating, and so was the university. Dean Lewis said that every student definitely identified as being among the snowballers on February 1 would be suspended.

Chief Harris was not optimistic that enough evidence would ever be collected to place definite criminal charges against any student. "College kids stick together and support one another's stories," he said. "Like police officers," he adds ironically.

The university police patrol Cumberland Avenue in every snowstorm now, but that is probably not necessary. The next "incident" of this sort will be at another university, and will be equally unexpected when it strikes.

The University of Tennessee's students did make the news again before the end of February, however. Eleven of them were arrested on February 23rd for breaking into Chattanooga National Park and stealing a

Civil War cannon weighing one-half ton. The cannon is federal property, and the crime is a federal crime.

Boys will be boys.

A few months later—on May 28th, 1965—the Grand Jury of Knoxville County convened and heard the case of the State against William Douglas Willett, truck driver, charged with homicide. After consideration, they refused to "return a True Bill," which means, legally, that the State had not proven an indictable charge. In other words, a case of felonious homicide "beyond a reasonable doubt" was not supported by the facts. In effect, this verdict meant that Willett must be presumed, legally, to have shot in defense of his life. The truck driver walked out of court a free man, if any man is ever free.

And there it ended.

Why did it all happen? One can only answer as German Chancellor Bethmann Hollweg answered in August 1914, when von Bülow asked: "Well, tell me at least how it got started?" According to von Bülow's memoirs, Bethmann Hollweg "raised his long, thin arms to heaven and answered in a dull exhausted voice, 'Oh— if I only knew.' "

It snowed heavily again this February in Knoxville—one storm covered the streets for a week, January 28th to February 4th— but there were no snowball fights on Cumberland Avenue. When death falls from the air again in this "meaningless" way it could as easily occur among a group of adults, or at a meeting of a government cabinet.

𝔍tem

Sir, are you using only half your brain?

Phil Gardner

You're pretty smart. We all know that.

You know all about partial differential equations, computer programming, cost analysis, flow charts, and vectors. If it can be put into an equation, expressed in human language, or recorded on a graph, you can handle it.

When it comes to the semantic circuit of the brain and precise manipulations of symbol systems, you're a champ. And everybody knows it.

But what about those mysterious right-hemisphere brain functions? Intuition? Synergetic apprehension of whole systems? Esthetics and ESP?

Imagine trying to live with one eye, or one lung, or one testicle.

Isn't it equally a handicap to use only half your brain?

"Specialization is for insects."
Robert A. Heinlein

"I once knew a man who was an ear, a magnificent ear, the greatest ear in Europe. But that was all he was: an ear."
Nietzsche on Wagner

Conspiracy

Digest

Interview 3

Conspiracy Digest: I tend to agree that your SNAFU principle is true for productive organizations. Certainly, I have seen exactly what you describe as the communications jam in the hierarchy while working as an engineer. However, the International Banking Conspiracy (in my view) plans destructive acts (destabilizations) through government coercion, which is much easier. Whereas individual initiative, as expressed in the free market, struggles to efficiently produce what people want, "bankster" manipulators seek only to disrupt this process by government regulation, spending, war, confiscation, fiat money, financed takeovers, etc. These disruptions cause swings in stock, bond, and commodity prices, on which the banksters can speculate successfully because they have prior knowledge of timing. They could care less if the trains run on time, but are prepared to make a profit by causing "accidents." Comment?

Wilson: The SNAFU principle doesn't apply just to productive organizations; it applies even more to destructive groups, like the Army (where, in fact, the term SNAFU was originally coined). The more

deception in a game, the more dishonesty, the more centralization—in short, the more hierarchy and authoritarianism—the more the SNAFU principle will fuck up its reality map. Far from being the superintellectual Machiavellians you imagine them as, the big bankers are probably (if my analysis is correct) the biggest dumb-dumbs on the planet. Every conspiratorial group becomes steadily stupider the longer it lasts. The paradigm isn't in *Illuminatus!*, but in Len Deighton's *The Billion-Dollar Brain,* where a Texas oil billionaire is trying to take over the world with the aid of a billion-dollar computer and a secret spy organization. Since every spy in the organization feeds back exactly the myths that suit this nut's fantasies, the billion-dollar computer (following the classic cybernetic law, "Garbage in, garbage out") comes up with a totally paranoid and bizarre world-reality map.

I originally got the idea for the SNAFU principle while reading Faulkner's *Go Down, Moses,* and I think I can paraphrase the sentence that gave it to me: "To the sheriff, Lucas was nothing but a nigger, and they both knew that; to Lucas, the sheriff was nothing but an ignorant redneck with no cause for pride in his ancestors or hope for it in his posterity, but only one of them knew that." Anybody who thinks he's in charge gives off a kinesic signal that discourages accurate feedback from others. Those who not only think they're in charge but use *guns* and *lies* and *prisons* and *terror* in general, get no feedback at all but the most outrageous lies. They feed on shadows in the absence of substantial truth.

Vlad the Impaler (the model for Dracula) once asked two monks what the people of Hungary really thought about him. One monk lied and flattered Vlad and said he was considered a stern but just ruler. The other gave him straight feedback and said everybody thought he was a mental lunatic who should be locked up. Which monk do you think he believed and rewarded? Which one did he denounce as a traitor and impale? Look it up!

CD: Nesta Webster in her *Secret Societies and Subversive Movements* claims that the inner doctrine of the Illuminati was (is?) antiauthoritarian anarchism: the destruction of Church and State. On the other hand, *Illuminatus!* and some of the Illuminati secret records (see Robison's *Proofs of a Conspiracy*) suggest that Weishaupt's real goal was (or is?) a new and absolute state tyranny (now achieved?). Was anarchism a cover for the Illuminati's real goal? Or was the Illuminati's anarchism sponsored by the International Bankers only until the ancient order of kings and queens was destroyed, making way for the bankster dictatorship?

Wilson: Beats the hell out of me. The only safe conclusion about Dr. Weishaupt and his buddies is that their attempt to maintain secrecy has worked marvelously well: no two investigators of the Illuminati have come to the same conclusion about the real purpose of the Order. My *Cosmic Trigger: Final Secret of the Illuminati* asserts that the real inner secret was that they had contact with Higher Intelligence in the system of the double star Sirius. I don't think that's any more preposterous than any other theories about the Illuminati, and I'll bet a lot of my readers believe it. The evidence is so good that I'd believe it myself if I didn't know what a great artist I am and how easy it is for me to produce baroque and beautiful models to fit any weird facts you give me to work with. Of course, as Nietzsche said, we are all greater artists than we realize; 90 per cent of all we experience is our own

imagination. In Stirner's metaphor, we have spooks in our heads. Nesta Webster had all sorts of spooks in her head (I always imagine her looking under the bed for Illuminati agents at night), but she was so modest that she didn't recognize herself as the artist creating all that. She imagined it was going on outside her. Blessed are the truly modest, for theirs is the kingdom of *maya.* I'm vain enough to know I'm creating my own reality tunnel; so I don't blame it on anybody else.

CD: I seem to detect what I term "virulent skepticism" in your views.

Wilson: Why, thank you very much.

CD: Although I agree that we must understand how subjective and mechanical the human mind usually is before we can even begin to approach objectivity, and must always be ready to throw overboard theories when better ones appear, you seem to be suggesting that a scientific search for reality should be given up entirely in favor of intellectual gamesmanship. Am I misconstruing you?

Wilson: You certainly are. At a rough estimate, about 80 per cent of my close friends are scientists. What I object to about political dogmas of all schools is that none of them are scientific propositions subject to verification or refutation. They are defined, it almost seems, so as to be beyond testing, and exist in the realm of faith, like theology or demonology. Conspiracy theories, in particular, are often defined so that all evidence incompatible with the thesis can be explained away as "part of the cover-up." The trouble with systems that do not admit of refutation, as Karl R. Popper demonstrates at exhausting length in several books, is that they do not

85

yield operational instructions for predictable technologies.

In this connection, my basic philosophy can be expressed as follows: the prosperous and growing nations have nothing in common politically. Some are capitalist, or state capitalist, some are socialist or mixed economies, some are communist, some fascist. The politics is obviously irrelevant to their relative success. What do they have in common? *Advanced technology.* And vice versa! There is no common politics among the starving, backward nations. Some are primitive capitalist, some feudal, some fascist, some socialist. What *do* they have in common? Backward technology or no technology. How, then, will we solve the problems afflicting this planet? Not by politics of any sort; all of it is irrelevant mammalian ritual. We will solve our problems by better, cheaper, more efficient technology; especially space migration, the technology of consciousness and intelligence raising, and life extension.

CD: In another interview (*New Libertarian Notes*, Box 1748, Long Beach, CA 90801) you indicated that there was some censorship of *Illuminatus!* What kind of things were cut out?

Wilson: The best parts, of course. All publishers do this to new writers; I think it's a remnant of some palaeolithic initiation rite, like having "Kick this boob in the ass" taped to your back after arriving at a new school. It also proves that the publisher is a tough, pragmatic, practical businessman who knows what the public wants, whereas the writer is a naive, artistic fool who'd starve without the publisher showing him how to write. This is very necessary to the publishers, since they are simple primates and need constant reassurance that they, by God, have the top perch on the tree. It is

well to remember always that we are living on the Planet of the Apes; *do not expect* intelligence, decency, or simple courtesy, except on special blessed occasions and with very rare and beautiful people. The average domesticated ape is only interested in protecting his own turf and his perch in the tree. You don't exist for him except insofar as you aid or hinder his territorial and status ambitions. Nearly everybody is controlled by the old brain and its mammalian politics; very few have learned to use the new brain.

CD: Perhaps the phenomenon you attribute to the "mammalian brain centers" is what I prefer to call the "pervasive dominant-submissive (sado-masochistic) conspiratorial order of human relations."

Wilson: Exactly! On Dr. Leary's Interpersonal Grid (1957), the sadist position is the extreme at the dominant end of the territorial axis, and the masochist position is the extreme on the submissive side. All this is built up on neural circuits that go back to the pecking-order rituals of the mammalian pack, and is quite robotic. People imprint these roles before the age of 3 and are still fixated in them at 23, at 43, at 63, or at 83—unless they are brainwashed into a new imprint, or become self-meta-programmers and learn how to "brainwash" themselves constructively. The self-meta-programmer adjusts flexibly to real situations and does not "play" the one imprinted position over and over. As Crowley points out, to attain that flexibility, you have to start by deliberately doing what frightens you most: going to the opposite extreme. If you're dominant, learn to come on like "gentle Jesus, meek and mild." If you're submissive, learn to bully and terrorize everybody you meet. After such experiments, you can gradually develop yourself from a total robot into a self-programmer.

CD: Although it would be comforting to believe that ruthless status-territorial-conspiratorial behaviors are instinctual and thus may be overcome by *reason*, I am afraid the opposite may be true! Perhaps the communal-tribal customs and bonds that limit competition to the productive and less-than-fatal realms are the mammalian instincts, and the more gruesome forms of competition and conspiracy are the product of *reason! Reason knows no bounds!* Many biologists comment that only men conduct intraspecies competition to the death. Doesn't reason *too easily* overcome the "gentling" imprint of mammalian suckling?

Wilson: Well, from my perspective, what you say is partially true, but inadequate. To cite my distinguished colleague Dr. Leary one more time, there are four major periods of imprint vulnerability in Homo Sap, the domesticated ape. The *first*, suckling imprint, recapitulates the biosurvival floating stage of invertebrate life, and is on a spectrum from trusting/loving/dependent to fearful/withdrawn/autistic. The *second*, territorial imprint, recapitulates territorial circuits of amphibious and mammalian life. The invertebrate infant mutates into a mammalian politician, toddling about the house and struggling for a "role" in the pecking order, on the spectrum from sadism-dominance to masochism-submission. The *third* imprint, activated by laryngeal-manual dexterity (human speech and artifact manipulation), recapitulates the palaeolithic age. The first circuit is roughly what we call Will, the second is Ego, and the third is Mind or Reason. At this stage, even if they're using hydrogen bombs instead of sticks and rocks, you're basically dealing with Stone Age characters. The *fourth* imprint, after the chemical releasers

of puberty, fixates a sex role and a socially bonded Adult Personality, recapitulating the process of domestication and civilization. The sad fact is that all four circuits are subject to bizarre imprints, robot rituals that make no sense at all. That is to say, the domesticated citizen of today certainly is more dangerous than the tribal character, because Circuit III "reason" is usually hemmed in by Circuit I phobias and anxieties, Circuit II emotional cons and mammalian politics, and Circuit IV sexual fetishes and moralistic terrors. Circuit III is also self-referential and never gets beyond its own axioms, in a sense. All creativity, in science as well as art, comes from higher circuits, even though at this stage of evolution it still has to be expressed in Circuit III laryngeal signals (hominid grunts) or manual symbolic graphs or maps, also Circuit III functions.

That's the bad news. The good news is that there are higher circuits forming. Leary had identified Circuit V as the neurosomatic or Hedonic circuit; it is generally called "higher consciousness" or just "being high." Circuit VI is where the real fun begins. Leary calls it Higher Intelligence or I^2, and Dr. John Lilly calls is self-metaprogramming. Gurdjieff called it the True Intellectual Center, and it is three mutations above the palaeolithic Circuit III, which is what most people mean by "mind" or the "reason." There are also seventh and eighth circuits, but they're irrelevant here.

The point is that Circuit III linear-symbolic reasoning is Stone Age and not fully human. As Jung, among others, has pointed out, people whose strongest imprint is on the third circuit (the Rational Type, as Jung called them) are absolutely as crazy as a drunken goat; e.g., Dr. Frankenstein, or Dr. Teller. They indeed know no bounds.

But the Circuit IV type, Gurdjieff's "Good Householder," although more promising as a possible candidate for Circuit V Higher Consciousness or Circuit VI Higher Intelligence, is *still* a domesticated ape, and usually terrorized at any idea that goes beyond either the local Circuit III reality map or the local Circuit IV moral code. The Circuit II types, or mammalian politicians, are, of course, totally hopeless, which is why Gurdjieff called them "tramps and lunatics." Reich called them *bigmouths*. Go to any political meeting, of any ideology on the planet, and you'll see that these mammals are in charge, or think they are. (Actually, everybody else, as pointed out by Hagbard in Vol. II of *Illuminatus!*, is always using sabotage, conscious or unconscious, to get around and undermine these Circuit II *alpha baboons*. That's another aspect of the SNAFU principle.)

CD: Since you are clearly an Aleister Crowley enthusiast, I was surprised to find no homosexual encounters described in *Illuminatus!* Were you limited to heterosexual "pornography" to maintain a wider appeal?

Wilson: Crowley didn't invent or copyright homosexuality, and his gay affairs are not the sole reason one might be interested in him. For instance, he was also a heterosexual, a masturbator, a mountain climber, a hunter, an explorer, a bad poet, a prankster, a great poet, a novelist, a high initiate of yoga and magick, something of a first-class amateur scientist, and a chess master. I happen to be interested chiefly in his works on yoga and magick, especially his philosophical writings. My own Agnostic Gnosticism is heavily influenced by Uncle Aleister, who once wrote: "We place no reliance / On Virgin or Pigeon; / Our method is science; / Our aim is religion."

CD: Illuminatus! appears to attempt to present an integrated "sexual-spiritual" theory. How does the homosexual "perversion" fit in? Clearly, this "perversion" has been a theme in secret societies from the Templars to the Hell Fire Club.

Wilson: I prefer the term "neurological" to "spiritual," because when we say "neurological" everybody knows what we mean, but when we say "spiritual" neither we ourselves nor anybody else knows what the hell we mean. *Illuminatus!* is, among other things, a precise manual of eroto-neurological techniques for consciousness expansion. This involves what the alchemists call sublimated sexuality—which does not mean repressed sexuality. Repression leads to all the neuroses, psychoses, and crazy chimpanzee trips chronicled by Freud and his school. Sublimated sexuality, in the Tantric and alchemical sense, is Hedonic Engineering, the art of getting so high that you fall in love with all sentient beings. Obviously, homosexual Tantra is the only form of Tantra that will appeal to homosexuals. I know virtually nothing about it, since I am heterosexual, but I very much doubt that it is in any way inferior to heterosexual Tantra. Some Gay magick societies have accumulated considerable psychic power. Different strokes for different folks, as the saying goes. Magick and faith healing are all based on Circuit V Tantric bioelectricity.

CD: According to Daniel Mannix in his book *The Hell Fire Club* (the influential eighteenth-century British Satanist club which Benjamin Franklin allegedly joined), they had "Do What Thou Wilt" inscribed over the altar on which they conducted Black Masses. Did Crowley get his motto "Do what thou wilt shall be the whole of the law" from the Hell Fire Club? Was Crowley a Satanist as claimed by Nesta Webster and other right-wingers?

Wilson: The origin of "Do what thou wilt" is Rabelais' Abbey of Thelema in *Gargantua and Pantagruel.* The Hell Fire Club was deliberately copying Rabelais. Crowley, of course, had read Rabelais and undoubtedly knew about the Hell Fire Club (which is more correctly called the Abbey of Saint Francis, by the way), but he claimed to have received the Law of Thelema ("Do what thou wilt shall be the whole of the law; love is the law, love under will") from a Higher Intelligence which contacted him in Cairo in 1904. Amusingly, the same idea also occurs in Saint Augustine, of all people, who wrote, "Love, and do what thou wilt."

Was Crowley a Satanist? Well, he could and did play the Satanist game on occasion, just as he played the Buddhist game, the Taoist game, the Hindu game, the atheist game, and lots of others. It is emphatically not true that his reputation as Satanist and Black Magician was spread entirely by his enemies; he collaborated gleefully in blackening his own character. To understand his motives, you must first understand the role of terror in reimprinting the nervous system for higher, post-terrestrial functioning. Aside from yoga and psychedelic drugs, the only method for reimprinting the nervous system is shock, especially near-death trauma. Most shamans are people who have gone through the death-rebirth process, just as in our own society you still find people who have passed through "clinical death," got revived on the operating table, and came back raving about transtime perspectives and beings of pure light. Crowley knew, as many shamans do, that you can get this result (shock and reimprint) quickly with some students by simply scaring the daylights out of them. A classic gimmick is to steadily increase their (repressed) suspicion that the beloved guru, in whom they have stupidly placed blind faith and love, is actually a diabolist out to destroy them, drive them mad, or enslave them. Crowley used this technique often, just as Don Juan Matus used it occasionally on Carlos Castaneda. The students who confront their fear and conquer it achieve a higher neurological awareness. Hagbard Celine uses several variations on this in *Illuminatus!*, and the same games were being played in the Eleusinian rites at Athens 2,500 years ago. The Wrathful Demons serve the same function in Tibetan Buddhism.

CD: What do you think about the Church of Satan?

Wilson: I think they're an amusing bunch of dodos, but no worse than the average California encounter group. I'm sorry to break up the national Hate Thy Neighbor cult that's so popular these days, but the path to awakening does not lie in expressing or glorifying the mammalian territorial emotions but in transcending them. I will say, however, that LaVey's gang are more honest than most encounter groups, in that they do deal with the Circuit II crazy chimpanzee unleashed by encounter techniques, whereas the others just invoke the crazy chimp briefly and then banish him back into the unconscious.

CD: Do you concur with Anton Szandor LaVey's theory, in his *Satanic Bible,* that Satanism has played a major role in European history and was the core doctrine of both the Illuminati and the Knights Templar? And the power behind Masonry?

Wilson: No. I will undertake, if anybody will pay for the job, to prove that the Hidden God of all the secret societies in European history was actually Bugs Bunny. With the documentary evidence as sparse and contradictory as it is for the persecuted heresies of Europe, one can "prove" anything by selective editing. Margaret Murray, for instance, has proven that the Hidden God was actually a Goddess (and most feminists believe her, of course). I think her case is better than LaVey's, but I don't believe either of them. Frances Yates' modest, tentative, and scholarly books, *Giordano Bruno and the Hermetic Tradition* and *The Rosicrucian Enlightenment*, shed more light on these matters than all the dogmatic tomes of all the ideological partisans. (I think the Hidden God was the student himself, or herself, after transcending submissiveness and seeing through the guru game.)

CD: Do you have any reaction to Dr. Emmanuel Josephson's theory that John Adams was the head of the Illuminati in America?

Wilson: As a historian Josephson would make a good dentist. John Adams was so damned independent that he couldn't even get along with the Federalists, the party he helped to found. When his son, John Quincy Adams, got kicked out of the Federalist party, old John wrote that he no longer considered himself a Federalist and hadn't for years. Even at the Continental Congress, where John was more conciliatory and less cranky than usual, he managed to offend everybody at least once. I can't imagine that crusty old Massachusetts farmer lasting more than six months in any conspiracy before he'd get thrown out for intransigence. Anyway, all the literature of that period points to Jefferson as the Illuminati agent in our government, if there was one.

CD: Although Josephson's theories of the Illuminati in America (to say nothing of his theories of the Skoptsi in Russia) are far out, I think you are giving him short shrift. Although quick to jump to dogmatic conclusions, he is one of the few conspiracy theorists to develop a competing conspiracy model rather than the timeworn monolithic model. His theory of the role of the Rockefeller/Rothschild (Standard Oil/Royal Dutch Shell) battle for oil in World Wars I and II is quite plausible in my view (see *Rockefeller Internationalist*). As historians, respected Establishmentarians and Fabians are good eye doctors (as was Josephson). Establishment-Fabian types (Toynbee and Wells) usually forget that people, no less conspirators, are a factor!

Wilson: Well, my estimate would be that Establishment historians are about 99 per cent prejudice, and Josephson was maybe only 80 per cent prejudice. History is one of the far-out arts in which there are almost no rules that a simple-minded novelist like me tries to follow. Frankly, the reason I don't believe historians is because the characters they create are too corny for novels: tinhorn villains and superheroes who belong in comic books. It's all war propaganda, before or after the fact. I have been on the scene of several important historical events circa 1952–1980, and never once did the press (Establishment or Underground) report what my nervous system sensed. Trying to find out what the hell is really going on behind the blizzard of lies put out by the 24 chief conspiracies on this planet is hard work, long hours, and low pay; and if by chance you do find out part of it, the fanatics of every ideology will jump all over you with spiked heels. Incidentally, Pound, who is generally considered even more of a nut than Josephson, was probably at least partially right in emphasizing that wars are often provoked to establish debt, i.e., to increase the profits of your favorite villains, the International Bankers. But there are other forms of predation besides oil competitions and money swindles, and all of them are, as Gurdjieff knew, "astrologically" controlled. That is, when the endocrine cycles which primitive occultists identified with planetary cycles reach certain "hot" points, the mammals start fighting. It is our misfortune to belong to a mammal species with technology sufficient to make the fighting increasingly omnilethal. But this probably happens in the evolution from mammalhood to true intelligence on every life-supporting planet. We're only halfway through the evolutionary cycle of our star, and the more advanced forms are just beginning to appear in random mutants during the past few thousand years.

91

Item

THE PARATHEO-ANAMETAMYSTIKHOOD OF ERIC ESOTERIC (POEE)
A Non-prophet Irreligious Disorganization

American Anarchist Association

⊂~~↵ "LEADERSHIP MEANS TAXES" ↵~~⊃

THE ERISIAN MOVEMENT   **HOUSE OF APOSTLES OF ERIS**

(X) Official Business   ( ) Surreptitious Business   ( ) Page 1 of __1__ pages

Official Discordian Document Number (if applicable): ODD#2b;iii/V;60EM3134

( ) The Golden Apple Corps   (xx) House of Disciples of Discordia; the Bureaucracy, Bureau of: Self-

( ) Council of Episkoposos; Office of High Priesthood, Sect of the POEE   ( ) Drawer O   Reflexiveness

Today's DATE: 60 EM, 3134   (1968 pagan)   **Yesterday's DATE:** 59 EM, 3134

Originating CABAL: Kount Korzybski Kommemorative Kabal

TO: Dr. S.I. Hayakawa

It has lately come to Our ears that you frequently and conspicuously pronounce sentences in public having an "is of identity" followed by a "snarl word"; e.g., "These students are fascists," "These students are crazed by dope," etc.

A scientific discipline known as General Semantics teaches that such sentences have detrimental effects on the nervous system of the user, contribute to neurosemantic disorientation, create confusion between the map and the territory, and lead to unsane behavior. A person habitually addicted to such sentences imitates animals in his nervous reactions, becomes dogmatic and categorical, loses the characteristically human consciousness of abstracting, and may even become so impassioned by neurosemantic primitive reactions as to commit crimes against property, such as attacking other people's trucks, tearing up other people's wires, etc.

There have been several excellent teachers of General Semantics abroad in the land during recent decades, and one of them, coincidentally, has the same name as you; if We were not aware that "the label is not the thing;" We might even think he was you. By further coincidence, this man when last heard of was also at San Francisco State College. We suggest earnestly that you should attempt to get in touch with him, if he can still be reached, and obtain from him some basic training in General Semantics principles.

He might also teach you something about neurosemantic relaxation. In the last photograph We saw of you confronting the dissidents, your entire face, shoulders, and body showed rigidity, neurosemantic "closedness," and the general nonverbal message, "Don't talk to me; my mind is made up." General Semantics might also teach you how to grow out of this infantile and primitive attitudinal set and function as a time-binding and open personality. Please get in touch with the other Dr. Hayakawa and give this a try.

Goddess bless you,

"This Statement is False"
   (courtesy of POEE)

Theophobia

Theophobia the Elder, TLETC

Kallisti ∞∞∞∞∞ **Hail Eris** ∞∞∞∞∞ **All Hail Discordia**

𝔍tem

The Eight Basic Loser Scripts

I. The biosurvival loser:

"I don't know how to defend myself."

II. The emotional-territorial loser:

"They all intimidate me."

III. The semantic loser:

"I can't solve my problems."

IV. The sociosexual loser:

"Everything I like is illegal, immoral, or fattening."

V. The neurosomatic loser:

"I can't help the way I feel."

VI. The metaprogramming loser:

"Why do I have such lousy luck?"

VII. The neurogenetic loser:

"Evolution is blind and impersonal."

VIII. The neuroatomic loser:

"I'm not psychic, and I doubt that anyone is."

Beyond Theology
The Science of Godmanship

One day in 1909, Dr. Sigmund Freud and Dr. Carl Jung were arguing about extrasensory perception. Freud — I imagine him with the inevitable cigar clenched between his teeth — was insisting that all that stuff was nonsense, and Jung was arguing that there was something in it, really, although he didn't know what. As the argument heated up and the emotional energy began to crackle, there suddenly came an explosive *bang* from Freud's bookcase.

"There," said Jung, "that is an example of a so-called catalytic phenomenon."

"Oh, come!" Freud exclaimed. "That is sheer bosh!"

"It is not," Jung replied firmly, feeling possessed by an intuitive conviction he could not understand. "You are mistaken, Herr Professor. *And to prove my point, I now predict that in a moment there will be another loud report!*"

No sooner had Jung spoken, than the same detonation went off again in the bookcase. Freud looked so aghast that Jung, who was a bit unsettled himself, dropped the subject at once. In his autobiography, Jung says he and Freud never discussed the incident again.

What are we to make of such a yarn? The skeptic will label it "mere coincidence" — or, even more strongly, "sheer coincidence" — and forget about it. This does not really satisfy anybody but the skeptic himself, and leaves most of us thinking of Ring Lardner's immortal line: *"Shut up,"* he *explained.*

Parapsychologists will offer two alternative pseudoexplanations. Some of them will say that the bangs might have been caused by something as banal as seismic tremors in the earth or traffic in the street, and the paranormal aspect of the incident was just that Jung suddenly exhibited *precognition*, the ability to see ahead in time. Other parapsychologists will suggest instead that what happened was *psychokinesis* (PK), what laymen call "mind over matter." According to this theory, Jung's unconscious somehow *made* the second explosion happen. Those who believe in this explanation say it also accounts for poltergeists (a German word for "noisy ghosts"), who allegedly afflict some houses with crashes and bangs for months on end, and even make the furniture fly. The noisy ghost, they say, is emotional-psychic energy accidentally unleashed by one of the people living in the house.

The trouble with these explanations is that, like *coincidence*, they are only words. The term *precognition* does not tell us what any scientist would want to know, which is *how* Jung saw ahead in time. And the word *psychokinesis* does not tell us *how* Jung's mind caused the second boom.

But there *is* an explanation for it, and for all the other paranormal events you've read about: the spoon bending, the out-of-body

94

experiences, the faith healers, even the eyes of Laura Mars. And the explanation lies in physics.

"I am inclined to believe in telepathy," Albert Einstein once said, "but I suspect it has more to do with physics than with psychology." When Einstein said this back in the Twenties, nobody in either physics or psychology understood what he was suggesting. Today, new breakthroughs in a far-out branch of physics called Quantum Theory indicate that Einstein was, as usual, fifty years ahead of his contemporaries.

These new discoveries seem to offer a single scientific explanation for all the weird events that parapsychologists have classified under such conflicting labels as ESP, direct-brain perception, clairvoyance, distant viewing, psychokinesis, out-of-body experience, and cosmic consciousness (Illumination).

What some physicists are suggesting is that all such mystical brain functions are aspects of one phenomenon: a subatomic but universal intelligence system that receives, integrates, and transmits information at a level much deeper than the sensory appearances of what we call space, time, and separateness. And this intelligence system, although outside spacetime as we know it, manifests itself within space and time as electrons, atoms, molecules, cells, complicated critters like you and me, planets, stars, and whole galaxies.

So, what is quantum mechanics? A quantum is a unit of action, just as a foot is a unit of length or a gram is a unit of weight.

Quantum physics first appeared as a theory in the 1890s, when Philipp Lenard observed that light travels in distinctly timed, choppy units like the beats of a drum, not in smooth, continuous waves like the singing of a violin. These distinct units are called quanta; the single unit is a quantum; and quantum theory is the body of experiment and mathematics dealing with such discontinuous actions. Furthermore, it is now known that all subatomic events occur in this quantum, or jumpy manner—a miniature psychedelic light show.

If the world of large things seen by our senses is like a straight line (———), the quantum world is like a dotted line (-------). Or, to employ three artistic analogies, a painter would describe the quantum world as collage, not portrait. A musician would call it staccato, not legato. A filmmaker would say it was montage, not linear narrative.

No cause-and-effect relationship has yet been found between one quantum action and the next. Most physicists are convinced that there is no cause and effect on that level. It is as if Law and Order function only above the atomic level; inside the atom, the surrealists, crapshooters, and anarchists have taken over the shop.

To the ordinary citizen, everything in modern physics is as queer as a three-legged duck anyway, and this lack of causality in the quantum wonderland is no stranger than anything else physicists tell us. To the physicists themselves, quantum mechanics has done to traditional science what Sitting Bull did to George Armstrong Custer. One of the greatest quantum physicists, Nobel Laureate Erwin Schrödinger, was so distressed by his own equations that he denounced "this damned quantum jumping" (*verdammte Quantumspringerei*) in a letter to Einstein. Science, you see, is supposed to be able to yield accurate predictions, based on the iron law of cause and effect; and the breakdown of causality within the atom makes it look as if science itself may be an arbitrary human attempt to *impose* order on a disorderly or chaotic universe.

Rising from the wreckage of causality, three lines of thought have attempted to make sense of the seemingly senseless facts. These are known as the Copenhagen interpretation, the multiple-universe model, and the hidden-variable theory.

The Copenhagen Interpretation was devised in the Twenties by Nobel Laureate Niels Bohr and named after his hometown, where he lived in the middle of the Carlsberg brewery, in a house given him by the crown. (Yes, Virginia, the commercials are true: Carlsberg really is the official brewer for the King of Denmark.)

The breakdown of causality in quantum mechanics is expressed mathematically in the concept of "the collapse of the state vector." You don't need to know what that means technically: roughly, a vector is a mathematical expression telling you the direction and magnitude of a force. It is enough to know that in ordinary (large-scale) mechanics, the vector tells you what *will* happen next, and in quantum mechanics, the state vector only tells you what *might* happen next. There is thus a great gaping hole between what science should be able to predict and what quantum theory does allow us to predict, and it is a hole big enough to fly a 747 through.

Bohr filled in the hole by saying the collapse of the state vector exists only in our minds. No, that is not a misprint, and, no, I am not oversimplifying. Another physicist, Bryce DeWitt, tells us bluntly, "The Copenhagen view promotes the impression that the collapse of the state vector and even the state vector (itself) are all in the mind." To the ordinary person who doesn't know the state vector from Finnegan's feet, this may not sound too alarming, but to traditional physicists, Bohr sounds like a man saying the brick wall you banged your head on is only in your mind.

Bohr was not a solipsist; he didn't claim the state vector was only in *his* mind. But his theory does seem, at least to his critics, to imply a kind of group solipsism, a notion that the universe known to science is not a model of the real universe but something once removed from that: a reflection of how the human mind goes about building models of the real universe. As Sir Arthur Eddington, an astronomer much influenced by Bohr, states this position: "We have found a strange footprint on the shores of the unknown. We have devised profound and elaborate theories, one after another, to account for its origin. At last, we have succeeded in reconstructing the creature that made the footprint. And lo! It is our own."

The Multiple-Universe Model has its roots in science fiction, and some physicists think it should have been left there. It is, however, a logical and consistent alternative explanation of what the hell collapses that unpredictable state vector. Briefly: everything that can happen to it, does happen to it.

This is also known as the Everett-Wheeler-Graham model, having been devised by three Princeton University physicists, Hugh Everett, John Archibald Wheeler, and Neil Graham. I don't know what they were smoking at the time, but this view holds, in effect, that if you toss a coin, it lands *both* heads and tails—in different universes. The state vector collapses every which way, as the actual quantum equations imply. We see only one result, because we are in only one universe; but in the universe next door, another you and another I will see a different result. And there are an incredible number of such *possible* (and by this fundamentalist reading of quantum math, *real*) alternative universes.

As Bryce DeWitt has written in *Physics Today*: "I still recall vividly the shock I experienced on first encountering this multiworld concept. The idea of 10^{100+} slightly imperfect copies of oneself constantly splitting into further copies... is not easy to reconcile with common sense." Indeed it is not, but DeWitt and others have accepted it as the least absurd way out of the quantum uncertainty problem.

If you can deal with the idea that in the universe next door, Hitler is remembered as a popular artist who never went into politics, and in the next universe over, John F. Kennedy decided not to go to Dallas on November 22, 1963, and lived to a ripe old age; and in another universe, you don't exist because your parents never met—you can take the multiworld path out of quantum anarchy. Otherwise, it is back to Copenhagen, where the universe we know is inside our heads, or onward to the hidden variable, where space and time do not really exist.

The Hidden-Variable Theory was started by Albert Einstein, even though he never explicitly used the term "hidden variable." Nevertheless, Einstein was always annoyed by quantum uncertainty, and attacked quantum mechanics from every angle possible, summing up his view in the famous dictum: "God does not play dice with the universe." In 1952, Dr. David Bohm, then considered the most brilliant pupil of J. Robert Oppenheimer, showed explicitly that Einstein's criticisms of quantum theory were valid only if there were a *subquantum* level: a world below the quantum world. Bohm also showed that this subquantum world could be the hidden variable that collapses the otherwise anarchistic state vector, but only if the supposed variable functioned "nonlocally." This means, in effect, *only* if space and time do not exist as we think they do.

The trouble with the Copenhagen solution is that, however much Niels Bohr and his defenders may deny it, this path ultimately leads to the conclusion that everything we think we know is only a construct of our brains. Physics then becomes a branch of psychology; it tells us not what the universe does, but what our brains do in organizing their impressions into ideas. The trouble with the multiple-universe model is that, however elegantly it may fit the quantum equation for the state vector, most of us simply can't believe in skillions and skillions of universes—each as vast in space and time as the one we think we're in—where everything that can happen really does happen.

And the trouble with the hidden-variable theory has always been that nobody dared claim they had found any subquantum world, beyond space and time, in which the hidden variables could function.

Until recently.

"Your theory is crazy, but it's not crazy enough to be true."

Niels Bohr to a young physicist

In 1964, Dr. John S. Bell published a demonstration that still has physicists reeling. What Bell seemed to prove was that quantum effects *are* "nonlocal" in Bohm's sense: that is, they are not just *here* or *there,* but *both.* What this apparently means is that space and time are only real to our mammalian sense organs: they are not *really* real.

This was the first step toward solving the mystery of Freud's exploding bookcase and similar enigmas of parapsychology, but nobody realized it immediately. The next step came—as is often the case in science—from three sources at once.

In the early to mid-Sixties, Charles Muses, a mathematician interested in para-

97

psychology, Dr. Timothy Leary, the LSD researcher, and Cleve Backster, a polygraph expert who had been investigating ESP in plants, all proposed that consciousness does not reside in the brain alone. Rather, they all proposed that consciousness goes down to the cellular level, to the molecules, to the atoms, and maybe even deeper.

The first to construct a complete quantum theory on this basis was Dr. Evan Harris Walker, a physicist working for the US Army in weapons research.

Dr. Walker explains this theory in a paper written with Dr. Nick Herbert: "The hidden-variable theory of consciousness asserts: (1) there is a subquantal level beneath the observational/theoretical structure of ordinary quantum mechanics; (2) events occurring on this subquantal level are the elements of sentient being. This being the case, we find that our consciousness controls physical events through the laws of quantum mechanics."

That couldn't possibly mean what it seems to say, could it? Yes, by all the potbellied gods of Burma, it means exactly what it says: our consciousness *controls* physical events through the laws of quantum mechanics. *We* are the hidden variable—or parts of it.

There hasn't been a more radical proposition since the Psalms proclaimed (and Jesus repeated), "I said, you are Gods" (John 10:34).

Walker and Herbert have specifically applied this theory to psychokinesis—and here we are getting close to explaining Freud's exploding bookcase. Using an equation devised by Walker to predict the amount of quantum wobble that can be produced by the human mind, they have compared the results predicted with those actually obtained in one classic, long-range

investigation of the alleged PK function. The experiments were conducted by Haakon Forwald, a retired electrical engineer, from 1949 to 1970. *Forwald's results exactly fit the prediction of Walker's equation.* Subjects trying to control randomly falling cubes produced results as far above chance as they should have, according to Walker's math.

Dr. Herbert has carried this line of thought one step further. Director of the C-LIFE Institute (a conscious robot jobshop), Herbert is a soft-spoken fellow who dresses like Einstein did (or a Sixties hippie). He had developed Bell's Theorem into the idea of the "cosmic glue," which holds, in effect, that everything is the cause of everything.

The waters get pretty deep here, but fortunately the cosmic glue can be illustrated, with amusing accuracy, by an old Sufi joke. Nasrudin is out riding when he sees a group of horsemen. Thinking this may be a band of robbers, Nasrudin gallops off hastily. The other men, who are actually friends of his, say, "I wonder where Nasrudin is going in such a hurry?" and trail after him to find out. Nasrudin, feeling himself pursued, races to a graveyard, leaps the fence, and hides behind a tombstone. His friends arrive and, sitting on their horses, lean over the wall to ask, "Why are you hiding behind that tombstone, Nasrudin?"

"It's more complicated than you realize," says Nasrudin. "I'm here because of you, and you're here because of me."

In Herbert's cosmic-glue theory, every quantum event is here because of another quantum event, which is here because of the first quantum event. At this level, causality is meaningless, and Herbert prefers to speak of "influence," which acts every which way in time. All of us—past, present, and future—are bound nonlocally by the cosmic glue.

Dr. Herbert claims this is the only theory of quantum causality consistent with Bell's demonstration that cause and effect are nonlocal, and with the Einstein-Bohm claim that nothing in the universe is truly random. In case the full implications of the cosmic glue still haven't hit you, Herbert will tell you quite bluntly: "Consciousness, nonlocal in space and time, is the hidden variable."

You ask at this point, "If this is true, why don't we notice it?" Why, that is, do we generally feel that our consciousness is located in one place—a few inches behind our foreheads? The physicists haven't tangled with this problem yet, but there are answers to be found in anthropology and psychology. In the first place, not all people feel that the consciousness is necessarily in the brain. The Chinese have always thought it was in the center of gravity of the body, and their ideogram for "mind" literally shows a heart and liver, not a brain. Hindus and Sufis perform daily exercises of moving consciousness all over the body, from the toes and legs and torso onward to the top of the skull and back down again. In the second place, modern psychology has demonstrated that where and how we feel our selves to be is conditioned by childhood experiences, and is not based on any innate physiological seat of ego awareness. And, finally, parapsychology and the study of other societies records ample cases of people who have experienced their consciousness as far, far removed from the physical brain.

According to the cosmic-glue theory, consciousness is everywhere and everywhen; we experience it here and now only because we are trained or brainwashed to experience it that way.

"There is a sharp disagreement among competent men as to what can be proved and what cannot be proved, as well as an irreconcilable divergence of opinion as to what is sense and what is nonsense."
Eric Temple Bell, mathematican

Let us, as the Chinese say, draw our chairs closer to the fire and see what we are talking about.

The story so far: the parapsychologists have accumulated a great deal of strange data about wild, bizarre behaviors of human consciousness. Although they have labeled these strange experiences with many names, the data all seem to reduce to the phenomenon of consciousness acting as if it were not imprisoned in the brain, as if it could migrate elsewhere occasionally ("out-of-body experience"), or as if there were nonsensory openings through which information from elsewhere can leak in.

The quantum physicists, meanwhile, have found a subatomic jumpiness or randomness that cannot be reconciled with common-sense ideas of cause and effect. Aside from saying the whole problem is in our heads (the Copenhagen interpretation) or that everything that can happen does happen (the multiple-universe model), the most plausible theory that has been devised is the hidden-variable theory which, together with Bell's Theorem of cosmic glue, suggests that consciousness is nonlocal in space and time (not locked into the brain).

The hidden-variable theory is gaining ground because its central assumption of nonlocality (Bell's Theorem) has been experimentally confirmed five times since 1974. These experiments showed that two photons (light particles), once in contact, will continue to react as if still in contact, no matter how far apart they are in space, exactly as predicted by Bell's math—and just as would be true if Walker and Herbert are right in claiming that quantum events are controlled by a consciousness which transcends space and time.

In San Francisco, Dr. Jack Sarfatti, President of the Physics/Consciousness Research Group, has gone a step beyond Walker and Herbert. "Below the spacetime level of the universe we perceive," Sarfatti says, "is the subquantal world of minimum intelligences. Imagine them as micro-micro-*micro*computers. They make up the hardware of the universe and are localized in space and time." (Each is *here* or *there*, not *both*.) "But," Sarfatti goes on, "the software or programming is nonlocal in Bell's sense." (The cosmic blueprint is here, there, and everywhere; now, then, and everywhen.) "The hidden variable," Sarfatti concludes, grinning benignly over his Mephistophelean black beard, "is not precisely consciousness, as Herbert and Walker think, but *information*."

Information in modern science has a very special mathematical meaning, more specific than in ordinary speech. Without going into the math of it, information is coherent order, as distinguished from noise, which is incoherent chaos. Biological evolution is the gradual emergence of information out of chaos. To the biologist, it is information in the genetic code of the cherrystone that tells it to grow into a cherry tree and not a teakettle. To the modern sociologist, information is the roads, customs, and traditions that mold random individuals into a society. If Sarfatti is right, information is also coded into the quantum foam, telling it to grow into the universe of space and time we know.

Imagine that your brain is a biological computer, as most neurologists now think. Imagine further that all subquantal events are also computers — micro-micro-*micro*-

computers, as Sarfatti says. Imagine finally that the universe is also a computer — a mega-mega-*mega*computer. What Bell's Theorem means, according to Sarfatti, is that the hardware of this interlocking system of intelligent Chinese boxes — or computers within computers within computers — is localized in space and time; but the programming — the subquantal hidden variable — is everywhere and everywhen.

This sounds suspiciously like a definition of God, because God is, according to all theologians, just such a nonlocal programmer — omniscient, omnipresent, and omnipotent.

But if this information system is a kind of God, or a scientific analog of God, it is also you and me . . . and the lamppost. The information, remember, is nonlocal in space and time; so the whole universe and every particle in it partakes of the information, and is thus a cocreator of the whole, but on different scales. Is this not what the pantheists have been claiming for millenniums?

Currently, Sarfatti is attempting to demonstrate this interpretation of Bell's Theorem practically by designing a faster-than-light communication system (US patent disclosure #071165, May 12, 1978). Although Dr. Carl Sagan has pontificated that this whole project seems to him "at most a playful notion," there is already a patent search afoot because of rumors that one or more other inventors are trying to patent the same device. Sarfatti also claims an unnamed intelligence agency is very interested in this, and a nuclear engineer, who has not given me permission to use his name, claims that the Russians already have such a device.

(Faster-than-light communication does not contradict Einstein, incidentally. The Theory of Relativity says only that energy cannot travel faster than light. Bell's nonlocal information system, as developed by Sarfatti, does not transfer energy but only information [order]. What is interesting to the layman about all this is that such a device, if built, would function precisely as the brain does in those altered states of consciousness studied by parapsychology. It would be a model of the extrasensory circuits of the brain, just as an ordinary computer is a model of the brain's logical circuits. And Sarfatti strongly suspects that, whether the Russians have this or not, advanced extraterrestrial civilizations certainly do. When Sagan says that Sarfatti's hope of contacting extraterrestrials this way is "playful," Sarfatti replies that Sagan's attempts to contact them by radio represents "electromagnetic chauvinism." So there.)

In fact, Dr. Sarfatti traces his ideas back to his early adolescence, when he received a series of mysterious phone calls from somebody (or some *thing*) claiming to be an extraterrestrial computer and encouraging his interest in quantum physics. The calls terminated when his mother got on the phone and told the entity (whatever it was) to stop playing jokes.

To this day, Jack Sarfatti isn't sure what to make of those phone calls. "Maybe it *was* an extraterrestrial," he says whimsically. "Maybe they want us to tune in to the subquantal, cosmic communication system. Or maybe it was just a practical joker, as my mother thought. Or maybe it was the CIA's Operation Mind Control trying to stimulate certain lines of thought among bright high-school students who were planning scientific careers...."

Sarfatti had his first jolting encounter with Jungian synchronicity when neurologist Dr. Andrija Puharich published his book, *Uri*, concerning his investigation of the controversial Israeli wonder-worker Uri Geller. Puharich claimed that all through his association with Geller, he had also received messages from an alleged extraterrestrial with a computerlike voice.

UFOlogist John Keel, in his books *This Haunted Planet* and *The Mothman Prophecies*, tells of hundreds of ordinary citizens who have received similar phone calls, during the past 30 years, from computerlike voices with weird extraterrestrial messages.

My favorite of Keel's cases is a housewife who got the Zen-like rebuke: *Wake up, down there!*

According to Sarfatti, it is premature to attribute such clusters of eerieness to actual extraterrestrials. We don't have to say that a real ghost haunted Freud's bookcase that day in 1909. And we don't have to say that the phone calls received by Sarfatti, Puharich, and Keel's subjects came from literal extraterrestrials. Rather, the subquantal consciousness, Sarfatti says, was agitated nonlocally (beyond space and time), producing these effects within space and time. But the source of the agitation was, he says, probably human emotions and beliefs.

Dr. Brian Josephson, 1973 Nobel prizewinner in physics, has taken the inevitable next step. Analyzing the puzzling differences found in certain key atomic experiments during the Sixties — in which European physicists were obtaining one set of results over and over, while American physicists were just as repeatedly obtaining opposite results — Josephson suggests that the conflicting belief systems of the experimenters were influencing the test data by unconscious PK. That is, in the most literal sense, Walker is right in claiming "our consciousness controls physical events through the laws of quantum mechanics."

101

"My goodness, Toto, I don't think we're in Kansas at all anymore."

L. Frank Baum

Another part of the physics/consciousness or mind/matter synthesis is emerging in Palo Alto, from the research of physicists Russell Targ and Dr. Harold Puthoff, who have been investigating "distant viewing" for several years. "Distant viewing" is Targ and Puthoff's label for one particular kind of ESP, which they have found particularly susceptible to replicable laboratory testing. It consists of seeing what is happening at a great distance from where you are located — as in *The Eyes of Laura Mars*.

Targ and Puthoff believe not only that their work demonstrates the reality of distant viewing, but that everybody has the talent latently. They even claim they can teach it to anybody, however skeptical, and have a standing invitation to all skeptics to come to their laboratory and have a go at it.

As Richard Bach, author of *Jonathan Livingston Seagull* and one of Targ/Puthoff's experimental subjects, writes in the introduction to their book, *Mind Reach*, "It is too late now to burn their files; what they've found is already being duplicated and expanded in laboratories around the world. As I am coming to know more of the powers that I have, so are thousands of others, so will the readers of this book."

Puthoff and Targ explain all their results by Bell's Theorem, which they paraphrase as "parts of the universe apparently separated from each other can nonetheless act together as parts of a larger whole," which is Dr. Nick Herbert's cosmic glue all over again.

Saul-Paul Sirag, Vice-President of Jack Sarfatti's Physics/Consciousness Research Group, has his own weird tales to tell. Once, while involved in the Uri Geller investigation, Sirag took LSD to see if in that altered consciousness he could perceive the alleged extraterrestrial behind Geller. What Sirag saw was the head of a hawk, which astonished him, since Geller had never described the entity as a hawk. Six months later, this image appeared on the January 1974 cover of Sirag's favorite sci-fi magazine, *Analog*, illustrating a story called "The Horus Errand" (Synchronicity #1). A year later, Dr. Andrija Puharich, not knowing of Sirag's experience, claimed that Geller's extraterrestrial ally had often appeared to him as a hawk, which he nicknamed "Horus" (Synchronicity #2). Later, Sirag discovered that the face on the *Analog* cover was that of Ray Stanford, a Texas psychic, who also claimed mysterious experiences with Geller and a hawk (Synchronicity #3). Oddest of all, Kelly Freas, the artist who had drawn the cover, had never met Stanford and was not using his face consciously.

Like Sarfatti, Sirag does not take this (yet) as evidence of real extraterrestrial intervention. "Such synchronicities," he says, "are merely indications that Bell's nonlocal subquantal effects are occurring."

Or as Dr. Timothy Leary expresses it in conversation, "Your brain is created by the nonlocal subquantal intelligence Sarfatti and other turned-on physicists are describing. That intelligence is both centralized — inside the atoms of your braincells — and decentralized, all over spacetime."

"Oh, sure," Sarfatti agrees when this is reported to him. "By Bell's nonlocality theorem, if intelligence is anywhere in the system, it is everywhere in the system."

Everywhere... not just in you and me (which is flattering), but in the louse, the flea, the rock, and (worst of all) in the people we despise. For, as the Zen tradition has it, a monk once asked a Zen Master,

102

"What is the Buddha?"

"The one in the hall."

"But," the monk protested, "the one in the hall is a statue—a piece of wood!"

"That is so," the Master agreed.

"Then what is the Buddha?"

"The one in the hall."

Whereupon the monk achieved illumination, and I hope the reader does too.

"The Science of the Impossible," originally appeared in OUI *Magazine; Copyright © 1979 by Playboy Publications, Inc.*

The Goddess of Ezra Pound

by Mary Margaret Wildeblood

"**I** wish Mr. Pound would tell us what he believes," T. S. Eliot lamented in 1932. In *Make It New* (1933), Pound answered tersely, "I believe the *Ta Hsio.*" This would seem to settle the matter: Ezra Pound was neo-Confucian. We would expect this from Pound's admiration for Voltaire, Jefferson, eighteenth-century rationalism, modern science; his translations of the basic Confucian texts (*Ta Hsio* itself, *Chung Yung, Lun Yu, Shih King*); his absorption in economics, social justice, and Utopian plans to save the planet; his contempt for "Xtianity... a cult devised to make good Roman citizens, or slaves," for "Hindoo squiggles" and "Bhuddist vapors," for "all that goddam Xtian, Jew, Moslem buncombe," for "Taozers" (a word that looks like Taoists and sounds like "dowsers"); his unforgettable judgment in *Cantos 52–71*: "Shit and religion always stinking together." What other "religion" could Ezra Pound possibly embrace but Confucianism, the most ethical and least religious of all?

103

According to "Bontrager's Law" (created by Dr. O. R. Bontrager, University of Pennsylvania Psychology Dept.), "*Everything* is more complicated than it seems." This is also true of Ezra Pound's metaphysics. The Greek gods and goddesses appear so frequently in his poetry that the Thomistic *Hudson Review* has accused him of allegiance to "the bar-room neo-paganism of our time," whatever that is; he has compromised his monolithic allegiance to *Ta Hsio* by saying elsewhere (*Instigations*) that Ovid's *Metamorphoses* is "a Sacred Book" (in contrast to the Hebrew Scriptures, "the record of a barbaric tribe, full of evil"); the later *Cantos* are full of admiring references to various Gnostic and Christian heresies, especially the erotic-tantric ones; *Section: Rock Drill* puts the down-to-earth Confucian social-justice theme in distinctly second place to a more pagan exuberance:

How to govern is from Kuan Tze
but the cup of white gold at Patera,
Helen's breasts gave that *

In fact, Professor Schneider of Louisiana State University, in his book on Pound, has quoted evidence that the poet was deeply embroiled in "occult experimentation" since at least 1914; and Christine Brooks-Rose in *A ZBC of Ezra Pound* asserts that E.P. was "a practising occultist for 40 years." Prince Boris de Rachewiltz, Pound's son-in-law, has commented on the vast library of rare and medieval magick manuals that Pound accumulated over the years, despite his chronic poverty; this suggests unusual devotion to the theurgic arts

---

* Pound refers to a celebrated drinking cup said to be molded directly from the right breast of Helen of Troy and, therefore, the most beautiful cup in the ancient world. Decent government is important, he is saying, but a lovely woman is more important.

in a man so poor that he made his own furniture to save money and fed all the stray cats in Rappolo because he knew what it was to be hungry.

Even the *Ta Hsio*, Pound's favorite Confucian text, is not quite so rationalistic as other Confucian works; and the version Pound translated as *The Great Digest* in the death-cell at Pisa, 1945, was "edited" (in fact, rewritten) by Chu Hsi, the syncretist whose neo-Confucianism was largely Taoist-magickal-mystic in emphasis. (Joseph Needham regards Chu Hsi as largely motivated by a desire to create a Confucian-Taoist synthesis as a native Chinese alternative to the metaphysics of Buddhism then sweeping the Middle Kingdom.)

Hugh Kenner, a brilliant neo-Thomist critic with a marked penchant for converting every writer he studies to his own religion (his *Dublin's Joyce* even makes the bitterly anti-Catholic Joyce into a Thomist) grants that "the most important character" in Pound's *Cantos* is Aphrodite.

The Gracious Goddess, indeed, first appears at the end of Canto I, where Pound describes Her ("Thou with golden girdles and breast-bands / Bearing the golden bough of Argicida") and tags Her with the Latin label *Venerandum*, the strongest tense in the Latin tongue, only to be rendered in English by some such compound as She-who-*must*-be-adored; i.e., we have no choice in the matter; She is too adorable to be resisted. She is, in fact, like the *Tao* as described by Confucius in Canto 74: "What you can depart from is not the Way," "The wind is part of the process/the rain is part of the process." (*Way* and *process* both render the mysterious *Tao*, a glyph made up of moving feet and intelligence roots.)

The unforgettable description of Helen of Troy in Canto 2 subtly incorporates the mortal woman into the immortal goddess:

Let her go back to the ships, back among
   Grecian faces,
Lest evil come on our town, evil and
   further evil
and a curse cursed on our children
Moves? Yes, she moves like a god,
And has the face of a goddess,
   and the voice of Schoeney's daughters
And doom goes with her in walking
Let her go back to the ships, back among
   Grecian voices

The adjoining Greek puns—*Elenaus,
Elenarke, Eleptolis*—subtly weave in the
oncoming theme of Eleanor of Aquitaine,
compounding double meanings into a triple
ambiguity. (The Greek means "destroyer
of ships, of cities, of men," and contains
Helen's name within each term. There is no
way of "translating" this into English,
although Andreas Divus caught a lovely
equivalent in Latin: "perditrix naviam,
perditrix urbiam, perditrix heroam, nupta
bellum." The last two words, meaning
"wife of war," join Helen with Venus, bride
of Mars. We are seeing the dark, Kali,
"Black Goddess" side of the Lady in these
early chants.)

Eleanor (and her father, Guilliame of
Aquitaine, whose implausible brag of having copulated with 120 women in a night is
soberly recorded in Canto 5) brought pa-
ganism back to Europe in the eleventh
century. That the troubadours of Provence
and the singers of the Grail legend—both
of whom found shelter and protection in
her court—were writing in code has often
been suspected. The Tantric symbolism of
the Grail legend is unearthed in Jesse Weston's *From Ritual to Romance*—written,
Dr. Weston remarks in her introduction,
with the aid of an occult group still practising these Mysteries in England in 1908. (I
have never been able to decide whether this
refers to a pre-Gardnerian Witch coven, or
to the Hermetic Order of the Golden
Dawn.) The full decoding of the Grail Rite
is given to IX° initiates of the Ordo Templi
Orientis, and was knowingly employed by
Richard Wagner in the writing of *Parsifal.*
As early as 1916, Pound was aware, and
wrote in "Psychology and the Troubadors," that the "male-female magnetism"
was used as a "yoga" by the troubadors and
minnesingers; he quotes in this connection
Pierre Vidal's famous line, "I think I see
God when I look upon my lady's body
nude." (Eleanor's famous bare-breasted
ride through Jerusalem was not a "girlish
prank" but a deliberate magick act, bring-
ing the emblem of the Goddess back to the
symbolic center of the three patriarchal
religions of Judaism, Christianity, and
Islam.)

By 1936, Pound was familiar enough
with this yoga to speak not only of "magnetism" but of "energies that border on the
visible," like "glass seen under water,"
extending "several feet beyond the body."
This is not the kind of knowledge one ob-
tains from *reading* the troubadors, however
diligently, even for as many years as Pound
admittedly gave to their works. It is the
knowledge of an adept. Soon he was ob-
sessed with the teachings of Scotus Erigena,
who lived in the ninth century, and was dug
up and ritually condemned as a heretic during the Albigensian crusade of the eleventh
century, when the pagan culture of southern France was destroyed in a genocidal
fury Kenneth Rexroth has accurately called
"the worst atrocity in history, before the
invention of progress." Erigena, to Pound,
was most notable as the author of the hermetic *koan*, "All things that are, are lights."
Dr. Timothy Leary, no doubt, would call
this an expression of the Sixth Neurological
Circuit, the metaprogramming circuit

opened after the imprinting of the Fifth, neurosomatic circuit by Tantric fusion. Pound registered it as a "clean mentality... free of the Hindoo disease and the Hebrew disease" which otherwise dominated the medieval age.

Erigena's aphorism appears, both in English and Latin (*Omnia quia sunt, lumina sunt*), frequently throughout the later Cantos, from 74 to 110, and is often linked with two lines from the troubadour Sordello, both in English and in Provencal, of which, the English (or Pound's English) is

> And if I see her not
> No sight is worth the beauty of my
> thought

Like Vidal, Sordello is looking at the physical body, but seeing more than "Single Vision, and Newton's Sleep" can discern. He is seeing the Light of Erigena, the White Light of the Tantric adept. Similarly, in Arnaut Daniel's 12th canzon, Pound was struck by "*E quel remir contral lum de la lampa,*" and in his 1912 translation rendered this

> and laugh and strip and stand forth
> in the lustre
> Where lamp-light with light limb but
> half engages

The thought is that the Lady's "light limb" possesses its own luminosity; this stuck in E.P.'s mind and in the '20s a typically terse half-reference to it crept into Canto 20:

> And the light falls, *remir*,
> From her breast to thighs

Only the word *remir* (sending the really obsessive Pound addict to a Provencal dictionary) reveals the origin in Daniel's canzon. Again, in translating an anonymous Provencal *alba* (dawn song), he managed the tricky feat of keeping all the original rhymes in place while moving from Provencal to English, and simultaneously hinted again at the Tantric light mystique:

> When the nightingale to his mate
> Sings day-long and night late
> My love and I keep state
> In bower
> In flower
> 'Til the watchman on the tower
> Cry:
> "Up! Thou rascal, rise,
> I see the white
> Light
> And the night
> Flies."

In Canto 39, we move rapidly from the most unique portrait of subhuman, purely animal sex in English literature ("Girls talked there of fucking / Beasts talked there of eating / All heavy with sleep, fucked girls and fat leopards") to another dramatic epiphany of the Tantric suprahuman Eros:

> Fac deum! Est factus!
> Ver novum!
> ver novum!
> His rod hath made god in my belly
> Dark shoulders have stirred the lightning
> A girl's arms have nested the fire
> Cantat sic nupta
> I have eaten the flame

(The Latin: "Make the god! He is made! The spring! The spring!" "Thus the bride sings." The bride is being wedded to the god, in a fertility ritual which consciously employs the Tantric light energy to protect the crops. This is the oldest of all magick secrets: the flame that is eaten is the alchemical elixir.)

Even Pound's economics become wedded to this pagan vision, in Canto 45, where the main charge against finance capitalism ("Usura," a Latin term borrowed from Scotus Erigena) is that it destroys the sacrament of Eros:

Usura slayeth the child in the womb
It stayeth the young man's courting
It hath brought palsey to bed, lyeth
Between the young bride and her
   bridegroom
        CONTRA NATURAM
They have brought whores for Eleusis
Corpses are set to banquet
at behest of Usura

This is, whores rather than priestesses serve the Free Goddess in post-Calvinist culture; contraception and abortion are rejected, not on Roman Catholic grounds, but as "unnatural" behaviors to which the poor are driven (see Pound's economic writings) by the hoarding of money in bank vaults.

Growing more bitter, and lapsing characteristically into Latin and Greek, Pound goes on in Canto 46: *"Aurem est commune sepulcrum / Usura, commune sepulcrum / ELENAUS, ELENARKE, ELEPTOLIS"* ("Gold is the common grave / Usury, the common grave / Destroyer of ships, cities, and men," the epithets of destruction taken away from the Goddess and placed where they really belong).

As the Cantos progress into their last movement, the historical personages fade into the background and the Goddess comes forth increasingly. In the *Pisan* sequence (1945), She is usually accompanied by the Chinese ideogram, *ming* (from the *Ta Hsio*), usually rendered "intelligence." Pound,

looking hard at this glyph's elements—the sun and moon together—found more light than rational intelligence alone can translate. Erigena's "All things are lights" usually trails Her and these heavenly lamps by no more than one or two lines.

Canto 106, typically, spans the world in hymning Her ("And in thy mind beauty, O Artemis / as of mountain lakes in the dawn / Foam and silk are thy fingers / Kuanon / and the long suavity of her moving"); under Greek or Chinese names, She is one.

A cone of power is raised in Canto 116, and the poet's confession of failure is an indirect testimony that She has not left him, even after his rages and *Dummheiten*, the death cells and the treason trial, the 13 years in a madhouse: "I have brought the great ball of crystal / who can lift it? / Can you enter the great acorn of light? / But the beauty is not the madness / Tho' my errors and wrecks lie about me." This rises, in Canto 120, to Her most perfect manifestation, and that of the *Tao*, although neither are mentioned by name:

I have tried to write Paradise.

Stand still.
   Let the wind speak.
   That is Paradise.

(*Cf.* "The wind is part of the process," Canto 74.)

More directly, Canto 113 is a statement of faith that refutes eternally the notion of Pound as materialistic social reformer *only*:

The Gods have not returned. They never
   left us.
They have not returned.

"Above civic order, *l'amor*," he already mused in Canto 95. In fact, the whole mixed jumble of Poundian political economics—Jeffersonian, Douglasite, Mussolinian—has been put into perspective under the neo-Confucian mysticism of Chu Hsi ever since Canto 85, which introduces the repeated line, "The dynasty came in because of great sensibility" and the associated ideogram, *ling*, both of which recur again and again in the last section of the poem. *Ling* is not something that can be taught; it can only be learned. Pound renders it as "sensibility" (as distinguished from correct knowledge, right ideas, or other intellectual values). It might be called "orgonomic sense," if that Reichian term were generally known and understood. Confucius says, "It is like loving a beautiful person or hating a foul smell, also called respecting one's own nose." It is conspicuous lack of this virtue which leads to the general ugliness and meanness of usurocratic civilization, as Pound observes in Canto 100: "way repeatedly not clean, noisy, and your hearts loveless."

The dynasty (Yin, actually, if you must know) came in because *ling*, sensibility, preexisted it, Confucius said. Pound quotes this repeatedly, because he wants to make clear that he does not believe, like most Utopians, that reform of the world is merely a matter of getting his own politico-economic ideas generally accepted. The higher awareness, the subtle sensibility, must first appear, before "civic order" can manifest. This sensibility, obviously, is a function of *l'amor*.

Looking at this *ling* ideogram again, we find in the middle of it *ming*. The Chinese dictionaries will tell you what this means: a dancing shaman, or a fertility ritual. Hugh Kenner unambiguously translates this as *witchcraft*. It is hackneyed to say that religion preexists culture. Pound has gone further and tried to show us what kind of

Ming

Ling

Bottom of Ling

The male-female magnetism was used as a yoga by the troubadours.

Sensibility is not something that can be taught; it can only be learned.

108

religion preexists humane culture.

Writing in partial sentences (for greater emphasis: the missing words function by forcing the reader to complete the Gestalt) Pound defines the theme of the Cantos, near the end, in two wistful clauses:

for something not brute force
      in government
and
To be men not destroyers.

Those who think Pound's allegiance to fascist economics* meant a devotion to fascist politics miss the point entirely. There is no poem in English more feminine, more loving, than the Cantos; the celebration of the Gracious Goddess not only anticipates the ongoing *Yin* Revolution of our times, but is the most poignant repudiation of macho values written in this century.

MARY MARGARET WILDEBLOOD was a man named Epicene Wildeblood until the Novelist who invented her decided to change her sex. She has adapted well to the metamorphosis and has become an ardent Feminist.

Originally published in *GREEN EGG.*

---

* This was chiefly an allegiance to the idea of non-interest-bearing money coined by the State, as distinct from the current practise in which 72 per cent of all "money" exists only in bookkeeping ledgers and serves as interest-bearing debt for private bankers. Pound also liked the Corporate State idea of having the poets represented in Congress by two poets, the carpenters by two carpenters, the doctors by two doctors, etc., instead of the system in which we are *all* represented by *lawyers.* He was wrong about Mussolini, yes; and he was an idiot whenever he got to writing about "the Jews" collectively (or about "the Xtians" collectively); but he wasn't wrong about currency. His economic ideas are similar to those of R. Buckminster Fuller and increasing numbers of postindustrial thinkers.

Conspiracy Digest

Interview 4

Conspiracy Digest: Francis King in his *Ritual Magic in England* claims that L. Ron Hubbard, founder of Scientology, infiltrated a West Coast OTO lodge for the FBI. After destroying the sex-magick cult, Hubbard supposedly used what he learned to start his Scientology cult. Can you shed any light on this?

Wilson: Well, the way I heard it, Hubbard was a member of the Agape Lodge of the OTO in Los Angeles in the '40s, but he didn't destroy it. It was years later, when some tabloid dug up Hubbard's link with the OTO, that he claimed he had been spying on them, not for the FBI, but for Naval Intelligence. As for Scientology, I would agree with Kenneth Anger's judgment that Hubbard took the techniques used in the OTO to liberate people and turned them backward in order to enslave people. But that may be uncharitable. As the Sufis say, every organization eventually becomes a conditioning or brainwashing instrument. It could be that Hubbard means well, but Scientology has lasted too long and become monolithic and myopic. I think Crowley deliberately screwed up the succession in the OTO (so that nobody could prove legitimate succession from him, and there are now five competing heads), just to prevent that kind of rigidification. As we Discordians say, "Convictions cause convicts." Whatever you believe imprisons you.

CD: Alternative paradigms (or world views) fascinate me. Isn't what you refer to as magick simply a reflection of the fact that numerous paradigms seem equally useful in explaining our sense data?

Wilson: By God, you really understand it! The whole function of Crowley's magick, like Leary's Neurologic, Tibetan Tantra, and Dr. John Lilly's metaprogramming theory, is to experiment with alternative belief systems or models until you realize that holding to any one model is stupid and self-limiting. (Modern physicists discovered this independently by getting down to the quantum-energy level, where things are so complex that you need more than one model to make sense of them.) It's like the old Jewish joke about the guy who sits playing one note on the violin, day after day, week after week, year after year. Finally his wife says, "Max, for God's sake, other people who play the violin try different notes and make whole melodies." He says smugly, "They're looking for the right place. I've found it." Most people imprint one set of biosurvival strategies, one emotional game, one symbolic reality map and one sex role, and then stop growing. To understand Richard Nixon, assume that after his first orgasm created his Circuit IV sex-role imprint around 1925 or so, his nervous system never changed again. He was literally looking at the 1970s through a 1920s reality tunnel. So-called "future shock" is really present shock, because, as Leary says, the present is the future of the nervous system. Most people are still seeing/sensing a world that vanished around the middle of their adolescence. Women, who take a new imprint at each childbirth, are less rigified than men, in this respect. Which is why, as Faulkner said, to find out what's really going on, ask the women. See who smiles more often—men or women. It's the women, of course, and that's not all sex-role playing or flirtation. They smile more because they've got more sense of humor: they see the realities that most men are too blindly robotic to notice.

Addendum 1980: I was perfectly serious in describing Nixon as a man who imprinted the 1920s and continued looking at the world through a 1920s reality tunnel even into the 1970s. If one compares Nixon's presidency with those of Harding, Coolidge, and Hoover, it becomes obvious that everything that had happened since about 1930 was somewhat "unreal" to him. Thus, Watergate was a rerun of the Teapot Dome scandal; Nixon's economic policies were pure Hoover; even the search for "enemies" (the "enemies list") was a reprise not so much of the McCarthyism of the '50s as of the Palmer anticommunist roundups of the early '20s; etc.

This hooking onto the past is not restricted to right-wing mentalities. Marxists are largely hooked into the social sciences of Marx's creative years (c. 1850–1890); the *New York Review of Books* is a regurgitation of the *Partisan Review* in its lively days (late 1940s); and as for the "liberal intelligentsia," Alan Harrington has defined them perfectly: "They still think the hot intellectual issue of the day is Marx versus Freud."

An explicit example of this type of neophobia and palaeophilia occurs in *City Miner* magazine for Spring 1979, in an interview with the no-growth fanatic Gary Snyder. Snyder says explicitly, "But what I'm talking about is not what critics immediately call 'the Stone Age.' As Dave Brower, the founder of Friends of the Earth, is fond of retorting, 'Heck, no, I'd just like to go back to the '20s.' Which isn't an evasion because there was almost half the existing population then, and at that time we still had a functioning system of public transportation." In terms of the theory in this book, Snyder and Brower imprinted the 1920s as positive and are still trying to adjust the world to evolve backward into that 60-year-old reality tunnel.*

---

* At least Snyder is honest about wanting fewer people. There are only two paths to take in dealing with the hunger problem: create a better technology, as urged in this book, to feed everybody; or else go backward, and let most of the human race starve. My complaint against the no-growth people, chiefly, is that they are not as honest as Snyder about wanting fewer people. The no-growth program does mean *genocide* (letting most of humanity starve off, and shrinking back to Snyder's 1920s population level), and I wish they would admit frankly that such massive starvation is what they are proposing.

Grok: when people talk about "going back," it is really not very important whether they want to go back to the 1920s, like Snyder; or to the 1930s, like many a nostalgic liberal; or to the 1960s, like Country Joe MacDonald; or to the Stone Age; or to medievalism, like many Catholic intellectuals. The important thing is that "going back" is a retreat reflex on Circuit I. The neophobia is the same in all cases; the imaginary past into which various nervous systems are hooked may differ, but the fear of stepping forward into the future is the same as that of the child not willing to leave the mother, the security blanket, the original infantile biosurvival imprint.

It only takes 20 years for a liberal to become a conservative without changing a single idea.

Item

Bavarian Illuminati
This is a Magick Letter

The science of Neurologic is easy.

Humanity is trapped (temporarily) in static, repetitious neural circuits that create misery, conflict, prejudice, war, stupidity. There is no longer any need for this sad situation to continue. It is easy to reprogram the nervous system and thus to remove these static, mechanistic circuits (conditioned reactions). You can be anything you want to be, the next time around.

It is easy to reprogram the nervous system. Start with the so-called "Thoth" exercise of Gnostic mystics. It begins as imagination, but it does not remain imagination. This is what you do:

Imagine vividly the "astral" field around your body, as shown in Kirlian photography. By *imagination* and *will*, change this field into the form of a divinity: Christ, Buddha, Pan, the Great Mother, Krishna, Aphrodite, or whoever you like. It is easy to begin reprogramming the nervous system by such vivid imagination. Do the exercise at least ten minutes every morning and every evening for one week. Then, the following week, do the exercise for fifteen minutes each morning, after smoking one marijuana cigarette.

Acquire a tape recorder. Record at least 50 times the sentence "You can be anything you want to be, this time around." Add to it a sentence necessary to your self-development, e.g., "I can be happy, this time around"; "I can be fearless, this time around"; "I can be loving and patient, this time around."

Repeat the transformation into the God-form while the tape plays back to you these

> # In an evolving universe, who stands still moves backward.

new programs. Do it until you know, beyond all doubt, that it is no longer imagination, that the new program has been recorded in your neurons.

Read and study carefully *Exopsychology* by Timothy Leary, Ph.D., *Programming and Metaprogramming the Human Biocomputer*, by John Lilly, M.D.; and any text on "magick" or healing by Aleister Crowley, Israel Regardie, G. I. Gurdjieff, or Mary Baker Eddy.

It is easy to reprogram the nervous system by these methods. Send copies of this transmission everywhere, especially to newspapers and educational or underground radio stations. The power of this signal is magnified 100 times each time it is broadcast over radio or TV.

As the species evolves, as technology (the extension of the mind in hardware) evolves, as we extend ourselves in space, time, and consciousness, the nervous system must also evolve.

Conspiracy Digest

Interview 5

Conspiracy Digest: Isn't the pluralist paradigm encouraged by ruling elites? Isn't the paranoid paradigm liberty's greatest ally?

Wilson: To the best of my knowledge, having read history back and forth for four decades, no ruling elite has ever encouraged the pluralist paradigm. All power structures try to brainwash everybody into a single tunnel-reality, with State education, Holy Inquisitions, FBIs, Gestapos, Drug Administrations, etc., and anybody who questions that tunnel-reality gets the hemlock (Socrates, 4th century B.C.), burning at the stake (Bruno, 17th century), the bottom cell in the basement at Folsom (Leary, 1973), or some similar discouragement. "Communication is only possible between equals" as Hagbard Celine and I keep telling people, and no ruling elite is ready, willing, or able to receive dissenting signals from independents or mavericks. Once you accept a pluralist universe, you are logically compelled to accept a pluralist society—i.e., a decentralized, libertarian, or outright anarchist society—and no ruling class can accept that idea. Rulership only makes sense if there is one capital-R

Reality and one group of experts who know how to make it run.

I don't see paranoia as the ally of liberty or of anything positive, and I suspect you are using the word in some special sense. Clinical paranoia is a dysfunctional condition in which the victim loses all communication with others (signals contradictory to his fixed tunnel-reality being screened out) and gradually disintegrates into suicidal or homicidal rage. Like all other forms of monomania, it is of no help to the victim, to his friends and associates, or to society at large, and is just a tragic waste of brain cells. We should always try to have a tunnel-reality this week bigger, funnier, and more hopeful than we had last week, and we should aim even higher next week. Besides, paranoia is a Loser Script; it defines somebody else as being in charge around here except me. I prefer to define myself and my friends as the architects of the future. If David Rockefeller has the same idea about himself and his friends, well, the future itself will decide which coalition was really on the Evolutionary Wave: the Money people or the Idea people.

However, the skeptical paradigm—or, more accurately, the skeptical method, since there is no one skeptical paradigm— is most emphatically liberty's greatest ally. I doubt the dogmas of the Left Wing *and* the Right, of scientists *and* mystics, of conspiracy-mongers *and* those who claim there are no successful conspiracies. At the same time, knowing that every sentient being has a signal that might teach me something, I am ready to learn from all of those groups. I doubt myself most of all. (But I'm also willing to learn from myself, since I don't seem to be crazier than any of the other fanatics around.)

The conspiracy I dread most is the organized churches, which have so castrated education in this country that people regard themselves as educated (and have diplomas to "prove" it) without any training at all in scientific skepticism, logic, or elementary semantics. There is no real energy shortage, as you have often pointed out in this magazine, but there is a most dreadful and tragic intelligence shortage.

CD: We seem to have jumped to different wavelengths on this question! I agree that no elite encourages independent, diverse thinking and world views. However, the current Western elites do encourage their subjects to believe that there is no elite, that is, that the increasingly totalitarian state of affairs is just an inevitable accident, the unavoidable vector sum of impersonal societal forces, even the will of the people! Please recall that, contrary to the opinions of the radical circles you frequent, ordinary, moderate folk believe we live in a democratic, pluralist country. (In fact, this is what, with Establishment guidance, they see as the problem!) Wouldn't resistance to Statism be increased if people were more suspicious of their rulers? Before liberty can be secured it would appear to me that a much larger proportion of the population must become "suspicious" of those who propose that liberty be given up in exchange for security, "greatness," a "new deal" or some other conspiratorial chimera.

Wilson: Certainly. But chronic suspiciousness, or suspiciousness without a sense of humor, can be just as blinding and limiting as the naive submissiveness of the masses. One tunnel-reality is as limiting as another. We are all blind men investigating the elephant. You have to jump quickly from reality map to reality map, time after time, to begin to "see the Elephant," in the Sufi phrase, and realize how complex and funny this whole terrestrial drama is. For

All the signals are jammed because nobody knows where the real power is.

instance, I am firmly convinced that the money lords are not nearly as clever as they like to think they are (or as clever as you think they are) and that real control has slipped out of their hands, maybe as far back as 1918, as Buckminster Fuller has suggested. The real control, even more amusingly, is in the hands of people who, by and large, don't realize they're in control, namely the scientists and engineers. They generally feel weak, exploited, and abused by the money lords, and think the money lords still are in control. That, I think, is the great illusion of our time, and only Fuller and Leary and one or two others have seen through it. That, again, is the SNAFU principle in action. All the signals are jammed because nobody knows where the real power is.

CD: As a conspiracy theorist I certainly do not try to "define others as in control." Despite my wishes, whoever is in charge around here, it certainly isn't me! Don't we have to discover the realities of power before we are likely to be able to improve the situation?

Wilson: As Mong-Tse said, "A man must destroy himself before others can destroy him." Perhaps you put too much energy into resentment, anger, denunciation, and similar negative energy states, and don't have enough positive energy surplus to achieve your goals. Perhaps you are too impatient and expect "freedom to drop into your lap as a fairy's gift," as Nietzsche said.

As Mong Tse said, "A man must destroy himself before others can destroy him."

Perhaps you are looking on too small a time scale to see the grand evolutionary pattern of higher consciousness and higher intelligence ever emerging. Perhaps you are too attached to the superficial and temporary, and regard each setback as total defeat, without seeing that intelligence always wins in the long run. Copernicus couldn't publish in his lifetime, Bruno was burned at the stake, Galileo was condemned and placed under house arrest, etc., but the new astronomy finally triumphed over the Catholic orthodoxy. Dr. Reich died in prison of a broken heart, because he believed that those who jailed him really were in control and, hence, saw himself as a victim of injustice. Dr. Leary stayed high (through a sentence nine times longer than Reich's) because he knew that, even in prison, even in the solitary-confinement cell at the bottom of the maximum building in Folsom, he was more in control than his persecutors. He knew that because his ideas were creating the future; whereas the gang who locked him up can't even control the present, which is, in fact, falling apart all around them.

As I said earlier, the path of intelligence is all hard work, low pay, and a high probability that the fanatics of all ideologies will gang up on you. If a person can't accept that cheerfully, he or she should give up such a dangerous occupation, and join one of the coalitions of true believers or Establishmentarians. If any of the conspiracies really are as all-powerful as you think, it certainly would be the wise choice to join them, if comfort or status are your main concerns. We in the SMI^{2}LE organization accept that we are living on the Planet of the Apes and that, as Charles Fort said, it doesn't steam-engine until it comes steam-engine time. The stupidity, brutality, and banditry around us are what one should expect on a primitive planet with low technology and only a few hundred years of science. (As Gurdjieff said, "Fairness? Decency? How can you expect fairness or decency on a planet of sleeping people?")

Frankly, I'd find life a bore if I weren't playing for very high stakes in a very high-risk siutation. We do have the chance, now, for Utopia and even for immortality. If we who see this opportunity aren't smart enough, adroit enough, and fast enough to seize the chance, then we don't deserve to initiate the next stage of evolution. In that case, the age of the mammalian predators isn't ending, and we are deluded visionaries seeing a future that can't happen yet. The order of nature is nothing to be angry about. Meanwhile, until they shovel me under, I still think our side is winning and that the power brokers you worry about are a bunch of dying dinosaurs.

© *Copyright 1977*, Conspiracy Digest, *Box 766, Dearborn, MI 48121*

116

Dissociation of Ideas, 4

Ideas are the source of all technology, all wealth, all changes in the environment by brain power.

There are four sources of ideas: mechanical association, a la Pavlov; logic; experiment; intuition.

Mechanical association is simple, quick, and often necessary to survival (e.g., stove is hot: don't touch stove).

Logic can discover whether a system of ideas is self-consistent.

Experiment can discover whether ideas are always true, always false, or sometimes true and sometimes false (e.g., cold stove not hot: safe to touch cold stove).

Intuition **ALONE** can generate new ideas and associations, new technology, new wealth.

Note well that *mechanical association* can be totally arbitrary and false (e.g., racism). *Logic* cannot, by itself, discover whether a self-consistent system has any relationship to the sensory-sensual-existential world. *Experiment* is aimless (the experimenter doesn't even know what to measure) unless given a direction by logic or intuition. *Intuition* can be totally wrong if not checked by logic or experiment.

Item

Lawrence Talbot Suite

by Simon Moon

In my mad and werewolf heart
I have howled forty-two years away
In despair and hope: the bread
And wine of werewolf Mass.

In my white and crimson soul
I have sung forty-two years away
In folly and scorn: the flesh
And blood of werewolf Time.

In my cold and fevered brain
I have laughed forty-two years away
In measure of fact: the line
And square of werewolf Space.

Until defiance built of its own ache
A truth less tame than the truth of Death:
My werewolf heart has howled against
Both werewolf God and werewolf Man.

Until terror built of its own heat
A truth more wild than the truth of Life:
My werewolf heart is pierced at last
By the silver bullet of the Lady's gaze.

My werewolf flesh is lost at last
To the silver bullet of the Lady's lust:
I am the Beast the Lady rides,
I am the Stars within Her hair.

Celine's Laws

by Hagbard Celine

A s every thinking person has noticed, our national life has become increasingly weird and surrealistic. The waiting lines at banks and post offices are growing longer all the time, even though demographers tell us US population is no longer rising. The street signs more often than not say *WALK* on the red and *DON'T WALK* on the green. You can't get a plumber on weekends. Nobody has been able to explain the cattle mutilations yet. Every survey shows that the price of consumer goods, the number of violent crimes, and the eerie popularity of *The Gong Show* are ominously accelerating.

I believe I have found the explanation for these distressing trends. Needless to say, I cannot present, in a short article, all the evidence which I have accumulated in three decades of careful metasociological research; that will have to await the publication of my three-volume study, *Why Everybody Is Going Bonkers*. Here I can only mention the thousands of depth interviews, the innumerable flowcharts and helix-matrix equations, the vast files of computer readouts, the *I Ching* divinations, and the other rigorous scientific techniques used in developing what I modestly call Celine's Laws of Chaos, Discord, and Confusion.

Celine's First Law is that *National Security is the chief cause of national insecurity.* That may sound like a paradox, but I will explain it at once.

Every secret police agency must be monitored by an elite corps of secret-police-of-the-second-order. There are numerous reasons for this, but three are especially noteworthy.

National Security is the chief cause of national insecurity.

1. Infiltration of the secret police, for the purpose of subversion, will always be a prime goal of internal revolutionaries. This is an ordinary part of the spy-counterspy game. There is nothing Weather Underground would like better than having a few agents in the FBI or CIA, for the same reasons that the FBI or CIA would like to have a few agents in Weather Underground.

2. Such infiltration will also be a prime goal of hostile foreign powers, for the same reasons.

Please note that these are simple facts of the secret-police game, well-known even to the general public, the subject of many ingenious plots in popular spy films, and not particularly alarming yet. Nonetheless, the seeds of Chaos, Discord, Confusion, and Paranoia are already here, for the simple reason that once a human being develops the *habits* of worry and suspicion, he or she finds increasing justifications for more worry and more suspicion. For instance, Richard Q. (not his real initial), one of my interview subjects, became concerned, after ten years in the CIA, with the possibility of infiltration by *extraterrestrial* agents. He was eventually retired when he began to claim that demons in the form of dogs wanted him to assassinate Laverne and Shirley.

3. Secret-police officials acquire fantastic capacities to blackmail and intimidate others in government.

Stalin executed three chiefs of his secret police in a row, because of this danger. One of my informants claims that every president since the National Security Act was passed in 1947 has learned how to have sexual intercourse without making a single audible sound, because of the possible electronic eavesdroppers. As Nixon says so wistfully in the Watergate transcripts, "Well, Hoover performed. He would have fought. That was the point. He would have defied a few people. He would have scared them to death. *He has a file on everybody.*" [Italics added.] Thus, those who employ secret-police organizations *must* monitor them to be sure they are not acquiring *too much* power.

In the United States today, the super-elite that monitors the CIA is the National Security Agency.

Here is where a sinister infinite regress enters the game. Any such elite, second-order secret-police agency must be, according to the above pragmatic and necessary rules, subject to infiltration by native subversives or hostile foreign powers, or to acquiring "too much power" in the opinion of its masters. (It may even be subject, if Richard Q. was correct in his anxieties, to extraterrestrial manipulation.) And so, it, too, must be monitored — by a secret police of the third order.

But this third-order secret police (such as, perhaps, Nixon's notorious "plumbers") is also subject to infiltration or to acquiring too much power . . . and thus, with relentless logic, the infinite regress builds. Once a government has *n* orders of secret police spying on each other, all are potentially suspect, and to be safe a secret police of order *n + 1* must be created. And so on, forever.

Thus who employ secret police must monitor them to be sure they are not acquiring too much power.

In practice, of course, this cannot really regress to infinity, but only to the point where every citizen is spying on every other citizen, or until the funding runs out, whichever comes first.

National Security in practice, then, must always fall short of the logically ideal infinite regress which we have shown is necessary to the achievement of its goal. In that gap between the ideal of "One nation under surveillance, with wiretaps and mail covers for all" and the strictly limited real situation of finite funding, there is ample encouragement for paranoias of all sorts to flourish. In short, every government that employs secret-police agencies must grow more insecure, not more secure, as the strength, versatility, and power of the secret-police agencies grow.

For instance, a certain left-wing nation which has employed secret-police agencies for 61 years has now reached the point where the leaders are terrified of painters and poets. In another, right-wing nation infested with secret-police agencies, several purges have been caused by three practical jokers who regularly call middle-rank officials on the phone and talk in what appears to be a code. The secret police, of course, are no fools, and are aware that this might be what it in fact is, a form of anarchist humor; *but they can't be sure.*

What usually happens in such cases is this: an official receives one of these mystery calls, saying perhaps "Pawn to queen rook five. No wife, no horse, no mustache. A boy has never wept nor dashed a thousand kim." He knows immediately that surveillance upon him will be increased tenfold. In the next few days, while memories of all his mistakes, small bribes, incautious remarks, and other incriminating events haunt his imagination, he observes the increased surveillance, and begins to suspect even the most loyal of his subordinates of watching him with eyes that miss nothing and to give a sinister interpretation to everything. Within ten days, he usually attempts to contact a foreign government to seek political sanctuary, and the secret-police net closes on him.

By the same process of worry leading to more worry and suspicion leading to more suspicion, the very act of joining a secret-police organization will eventually turn a man or woman into a clinical paranoid; in layman's terms, "bananas" or "wigged out." *The agent knows whom he is spying on; but he never knows who is spying on him.* Could it be his wife, his girl friend, his secretary, the newsboy, the Good Humor man?

For these reasons, secret-police agents develop elaborate and complex theories to account for what is actually going on. According to one of my tables of data, there

isn't a single theory held by professional conspiracy buffs which isn't also believed by many members of our various secret-police agencies. In fact, the exact percent-

Table 1. True Believers in Various Conspiracy Theories Among CIA Agents and Underground-Press Readers.[a]

Conspiracy Theory	CIA	Underground-Press Readers
The Yankees (Eastern millionaires) run everything.	25[b]	30
The Cowboys (Western millionaires) run everything.	25	15
It's the result of a civil war between Yankees and Cowboys.	23	17
It's the 33° Masons.	5	5
It's the Jesuits.	5	5
It's the Elders of Zion.	2	2
It's the Military-Industrial Complex.	1	2
It's the Bilderbergers.	1	2
It's the Gnomes of Zürich.	1	2
It's the Lesbian Vegetarians.	10	28
Miscellaneous[c]	2	2

a. *Source:* Gallup, Roper, and Hogtied, *Who's Watching Whom* (Washington, DC: US Government Printing Office, 1979), p. 432.

b. All figures are percentages. Figures do not add to 100, for a variety of reasons. For a list of them, please send 25¢ and a list of suspicious persons in your neighborhood to the US Dept. of Bedding, Washington, DC 20001.

c. Includes those who blame it all on the Bavarian Illuminati; those who hold a multiconspiracy theory (e.g., the Lesbian Vegetarians are allied with the Yankees and Bilderbergers against the Cowboys, the TV Networks, and the Cattle Mutilators); those who believe it is all part of the UFO Cover-Up; and those who claim that demons in the form of dogs told them it's connected somehow with the alligators in New York's sewers.

ages of believers in these extravagant scenarios are quite similar among a group of 1,000 CIA agents and a control group of 1,000 readers of the underground press, as shown in Table 1.

In Russia, the government is terrified of painters and poets.

Now, Table 1 clearly gives a picture of a rather schizzed-out nation. This is the result of the impossible infinite regress and its resultant of worry leading to more worry.

Furthermore, if there is a secret police at all, in any nation you care to imagine, *every branch and department of that country's government becomes suspect,* in the eyes of cautious and intelligent people, *as a possible front for or funnel to the secret police.* (That is, the more shrewd citizens will recognize that something titled a branch of HEW or even PTA might actually be run by the CIA.) Inevitably, the government as a whole, and many nongovernmental agencies, will be regarded by reasonable persons with fear and trepidation. Proverbs like "One can't be too careful these days" and "Better safe than sorry" become a kind of sinister folk wisdom.

But further yet: any government which already has a secret police (and a secret police monitoring the secret police, etc.) will become alarmed on observing that its more hip and intelligent citizens now regard it with loathing and misgivings. *The government will therefore increase the size and powers of the secret police.* This is the only rational move, within the context of the secret-police game.

Something passing as a branch of HEW might be a front for the CIA.

(The only alternative was once suggested sarcastically by playwright Bert Brecht, who said, "If the government doesn't trust the people, why doesn't it dissolve them and elect a new people?" No way has yet been invented to elect a new people; so the police state will instead spy on the existing people even more vigorously.)

This, of course, creates additional paranoia in both the governors and the citizens, because a sufficiently pugnacious secret police will eventually "have a file on everybody," including its own creators. This leads to another infinite regress: the more power the secret police has, the more people will loathe the government; and the more people loathe the government, the more power will be given to the secret police.

Thus, whether any of the hypothetical conspiracies mentioned earlier really exist or not, a system of clandestine government inevitably produces, in both the rulers and the ruled, a mood of paranoia in which such conspiracy theories flourish.

This escalating sense of suspiciousness is accelerated by the fact that every secret-police organization engages in both the *collection of information* and the *production of misinformation.* That is, you score points in the secret-police game both by hoarding signals (information units)—that is, by hiding facts from competitive players—and by foisting false signals (fake information units) on the other players. This creates the situation which I call Optimum Fuckup, in which every participant has rational (not neurotic) cause to suspect that every other player may be attempting to deceive him, gull him, con him, dupe him, and generally misinform him. As Henry Kissinger is rumored to have said, anybody in Washington these days who isn't paranoid is crazy.

One could generalize the remark: anyone in the United States today who isn't paranoid must be crazy.

"If the government doesn't trust the people, why doesn't it dissolve them and elect a new people?"

The deliberate production of misinformation (or, as intelligence agencies more euphemistically call it, disinformation) creates a situation profoundly disorienting to the philosopher, the scientist, and the ordinary Joe who wants to know the best time to go to the bank. The desire to discover "what the hell is really going on" (the definition of science offered by physicist Saul-Paul Sirag) is totally incompatible with the circulation of disinformation; we all need to know, at least roughly, what the hell is really going on if we are not to stumble around like blind robots colliding with things we weren't told were there.

Maybe the UFOs really exist — or maybe the whole UFO phenomenon is a cover for an intelligence operation. Maybe there are black holes where space and time implode — or maybe the entire black-hole cosmology was created to befuddle and mislead Russian scientists. Maybe Jimmy

Carter really exists — or maybe he is, as the *National Lampoon* claims, an actor named Sidney Goldfarb specially trained to project the down-home virtues that the American people nostalgically seek. Perhaps only three men at the top of the National Security Agency really know the answers to these questions — or perhaps those three are being deceived by certain subordinates (as Lyndon Johnson was deceived by the CIA about Vietnam) and are as disoriented as the rest of us. Such is the logic of a Disinformation Matrix.

Personally, I find it easier to believe in UFOs than in black holes or Jimmy Carter; but that may just indicate the damage to my own brain caused by the Optimum Fuckup of the Disinformation Matrix.

According to a recent survey, 19 per cent of the population believe the moon landings were faked by Stanley Kubrick and a gang of special-effects experts. Perhaps these archskeptics are the sanest ones left among us. Who among the readers of this book has a security clearance high enough to be *absolutely* sure that these ultraparanoids are wrong?

This general tendency toward chaos, discord, and confusion, once a secret police has been established, is complicated and accelerated by Celine's Second Law, to wit: *Accurate communication is only possible in a nonpunishing situation.* This is a very simple statement of the obvious, and means no more than that everybody tends to lie a little, to flatter or to protect themselves, when dealing with those who have power over them, especially the power to punish. (This is why communication between parents and children is notoriously befoozled.)

Every authoritarian structure can be visualized as a pyramid, with very few at the top and very many at the bottom, as in the flowchart of any corporation or bureaucracy. On each rung, participants bear a *burden of nescience* in relation to those above them. That is, they must be very, very careful that their natural sensory activities as conscious organisms — the acts of seeing, hearing, smelling, tasting, feeling, drawing inferences from perception, etc. — be *in accord with the wishes of those above them.* This is absolutely vital; job security depends on it. It is much less important — a luxury that can easily be discarded — that these perceptions be *in accord with actual reality.*

Communication is only possible between equals.

For instance, in the FBI under J. Edgar Hoover, the agent had to develop the capacity to see godless communists everywhere. Any agent whose perceptions indicated that there were actually very few godless communists anywhere in this country would experience what psychologists call *cognitive dissonance*: his or her reality grid was at variance with the official reality grid of the pyramidal authority structure. To talk about such divergent perceptions at all would be to invite suspicions of eccentricity, of intellectual wiseacreing, or of being oneself a godless communist. The same would apply to any Dominican Inquisitor of earlier centuries who lacked the capacity to see witches everywhere. In such authoritarian situations, it is important to see what the authorities see; it is inconvenient, and possibly dangerous, to see what is actually there.

But this leads to an equal and opposite *burden of omniscience* on those at the top, in the Eye of the authoritarian pyramid. All that is forbidden to those at the bottom — the conscious activities of perception and evaluation — is demanded of the master classes, the elite and the super-elite. They must attempt to do the seeing, hearing, smelling, tasting, feeling, thinking, and decisionmaking for the whole society.

But a man with a gun (the power to punish) is told only what his target thinks will not cause him to pull the trigger. The elite, with their burden of omniscience, face the underlings, with their burden of nescience, and receive only the feedback consistent with their own preconceived notions. The burden of omniscience becomes, in short, another and more complex burden of nescience. Nobody really knows anything anymore, or if they do, they are careful to hide the fact.

As the national security paradigm approaches (or attempts to approach) the ideal infinite regress of spies-spying-on-spies-spying-on-spies, etc., the resultant general trepidation causes all persons to hide anything they know (if it differs from the official reality), not only from their superiors, but from peers and inferiors as well. *Anybody,* after all, might be part of the *n*th-degree secret police. "One can't be too careful these days." The burden of nescience becomes omnipresent. More and more of reality becomes unspeakable.

But as Freud noted, that which is objectively repressed (unspeakable) soon becomes subjectively repressed (unthinkable). Nobody likes to feel like a coward and a liar constantly. *It is easier to cease to notice where the official reality grid differs from sensed experience.* Thus Optimum Fuckup gradually becomes Terminal Fuckup, and *rigiditus bureaucraticus* sets in; this is the last stage before all brain activity ceases, and the society is intellectually dead.

Celine's Third Law is like unto the first two, and holds that *An honest politician is a national calamity.*

At first glance, this seems preposterous. People of all shades of opinion agree at least on the axiom that we need more honest politicians, not more crooked ones. Please remember, however, that people of all shades of opinion once agreed that the Earth is flat.

Your typical dishonest politician *(bocca grande normalis)* is interested only in enriching himself at the public expense, a goal he shares with most of his fellow citizens, especially doctors and lawyers. This is normal behavior for our primate species, and society has always been able to endure and survive it.

Nobody knows anything, or if they do, they are careful to hide the fact.

An honest politician *(bocca grande giganticus)* is far more dangerous. He or she is sincerely committed to bettering society by political action. In practice, that means by writing and enacting more laws. Indeed, many groups of idealistic citizens publish rating sheets on politicians every year, and those who have created more laws are estimated as having higher value than those who are frequently absent when bills are voted upon. The assumption is that adding more laws to the statute books is a positive achievement, like adding more money to our paychecks or more art works to a museum.

A little thought, however, shows that this assumption is not tenable. Every law creates a whole new criminal class; for instance, when marijuana was illegalized in 1937, several hundred thousand formerly law-abiding citizens became criminals overnight, by Act of Congress. As more and more laws are passed, more and more citizens become criminals. The chief cause of the rising crime rate is the rising number of laws being enacted. An honest politician, who keeps his nose to the grindstone and enacts several hundred laws in the course of his career, thereby produces as many as several million new criminals.

It is furthermore mathematically demonstrable that the more laws there are, the more restrictions there are on the freedom of the individual. If there were, say, only three laws in a given society — e.g., Thou shalt not kill; thou shalt not steal; thou shalt not lie or defraud — there would be only three restrictions on freedom, which all rational persons would accept as obviously necessary to the maintenance of order. When there are several hundred thousand laws, as in these states today, there are several hundred thousand restrictions on freedom, most of which are felt as extremely irksome by large segments of the populace.

In fact, it would take a brigade of lawyers several weeks, minutely examining your affairs, to determine if you are a criminal. Certainly, no ordinary citizen has the time or the research facilities to discover if he or she is in violation of one out of the skillions of laws currently on our statute books. In many cases, two lawyers consulted independently will give opposite opinions about whether or not a given course of action is in violation of the statutes.

And new laws are being enacted all the time. Obviously, unless there is a sudden paper shortage, the number of laws on the books will eventually reach the point satirized by T. H. White, in which "everything not prohibited is compulsory." It would then probably only take a few years or decades more for a cadre of honest politicians diligently writing even more laws to reach the complementary point where "everything not compulsory is prohibited."

Every law creates a whole new criminal class overnight.

At that stage the nightmare world of Orwell's *1984* will be achieved. Crooked politicians, merely interested in the normal human activity of making themselves rich and comfortable, could never create that ultimate horror; but honest and idealistic politicians bring us closer to it every day, with every new law they enact.

These three generalizations—that national security produces national insecurity; that authoritarianism produces miscommunication and eventual idiocy; and that honest politicians are a plague upon society—will be found to fully explain the Decline and Fall of Rome, the Decline and Fall of the British Empire, and the Decline and Fall of any country you care to name. They are as universal as Newton's laws of motion and apply to all cases. Of course, the American Sociological Association says I am mad. Mad, am I? They said the Wright Brothers were mad. They said Edison was mad. They said Baron Frankenstein was mad. . . .

BOOKS

Infinite Cruelty

by Epicene Wildeblood

At the age of 30, Raymond Chandler, an American raised in England and thoroughly imprinted with the stoic code of the English Public School, found himself a platoon commander in World War I. For nearly a decade Chandler had been struggling to establish himself as a writer and had gotten nowhere, for excellent reasons: his peotry was ninth-rate imitation Swinburne and his essays were even worse. Now, suddenly separated from what was then called literature, he found himself confronting life and death. Specifically, he led several charges against German machine-gun fire.

"Courage is a strange thing: one can never be sure of it," he wrote in a letter years later. "As a platoon commander very many years ago I never seemed afraid, and yet I have been afraid of the most insignificant risks." Warming to the subject, Chandler discussed the psychology of moving forward against a machine-gun nest: "If you had to go over the top, somehow all you seemed to think of was trying to keep the men spaced, in order to reduce casualties. It was always very difficult, especially if you had replacements or men who had been wounded. It's only human to want to bunch together for companionship in the face of heavy fire."

One day in Hollywood in the 1950s, when Chandler had become rich and famous and the Black List was speaking louder than the Box Office about who would get hired next year, J. Edgar Hoover found himself in a restaurant at which Chandler was dining. Hoover sent a message via a waiter that he would like to speak to the most famous detective-story writer in the country. Chandler's reply was terse and typical: "Tell Mr. J. Edgar Hoover to go to hell."

That's what an English education will do for you: Chandler wouldn't forget the "Mr." even when telling a man to go to hell; but he would offer no other meed of good manners to a thug like Hoover, even if Presidents of the US or really powerful presidents of film studios quaked before Hoover's wrath.

People who met Raymond Chandler after he became a celebrity always commented that he was nothing like the hero of his novels, Philip Marlowe. Frank MacShane's *Life of Raymond Chandler* (1978) makes amply clear how wrong they all were. Chandler at 5'11" was an inch and a half shorter than Marlowe; he wore glasses and, it was usually said, "talked like a professor"—which is to say that he talked like what he was, an English Public School graduate who had majored in classics. Underneath these superficialities, Chandler was Marlowe and Marlowe was Chandler. The man who told J. Edgar Hoover to go to hell in the witch-hunting '50s was the man who, in the novels, is willing to fight alone for his own concept of decency against oil millionaires, Hollywood producers, corrupt cops, crooked DAs, and the whole power apparatus which has made southern

California the wealthiest right-wing enclave outside Dallas.

It took Chandler a long time to create Marlowe. Like Pound's Hugh Selwyn Mauberley, Chandler found that WWI "destroyed in him / the artist's urge." He stopped writing his Romantic poetry—what the hell did that have to do with the world he had seen in the war?—and returned to the land of his birth, where he didn't write a line for 15 years. Instead, he deliberately mutated himself from an English esthete into an American businessman: no small feat of neurological reprogramming. That he succeeded until the age of 45 is astonishing in itself; that he became a major executive in three oil firms reminds one of Paul Gauguin, another artist who spent most of his life in flight from art.

As Chandler later wrote, "I have spent my life on the edge of nothing"—and, in another place, he added, "Once you have had to lead a platoon into direct machine-gun fire, nothing is ever the same again." He had a vision of a world that was made of glass, a world where anyone could be smashed in an instant, carelessly or maliciously as the case might be, but in any case shattered beyond repair: no literary technique existed to convey that vision. Chandler spent 15 years, the prime years of a man's life, in the oil-executive game before the Daemon or Holy Guardian Angel that haunts artists got its teeth into him again. Typically, the first symptoms were pathological: he became an alcoholic, and seems to have made a career of it. MacShane makes abundantly clear that because of his excellent previous record, Chandler was given a great deal of tolerance before the patience of his Board of Directors was exhausted. He was only fired after several monumental benders in which he stayed drunk for weeks on end without coming anywhere near the office.

At the age of 45, with a vain and expensive wife, no job, and a heavy alcohol habit, Chandler had no place to go but up. He stopped drinking and started writing again, and in a few years he had created the unique

> # The emotional impact of Chandler's books depends on physiological sensations and neurological nuances.

literary form which is his and his alone, although more widely counterfeited than any other technique but Hemingway's. It was a kind of detective story that had never existed before, not even in the bitter and bloody pages of Dashiell Hammett; some purists of the logical-deductive tale even claimed it wasn't a detective story at all.

What Chandler had invented, as Edmund Wilson was the first to note, is akin to the espionage novels of Eric Ambler and Graham Greene, in which "it is not simply a question here of a puzzle which has been put together but of a malaise conveyed to the reader, the horror of a hidden conspiracy which is continually turning up in the most varied and unlikely forms." *Farewell, My Lovely*—a Romantic title for a horrid story—begins with a seemingly senseless murder in Los Angeles's Black ghetto, but as Marlowe investigates, the reader is led step-by-step into every aspect of southern California life, from the mansions of the very rich to the gambling casinos run by the Mafia, and the "hidden conspiracy" is everywhere. Chandler had learned a lot in the oil business, and the links between rich men with fine manners and delicate sensibilities down through corrupt politicians and crooked cops to outright hoodlums and psychopaths are traced with clinical accuracy, foreshadowing newspaper exposes that didn't appear until 30 years after Chandler's earliest novels. His world is indeed the claustrophobic landscape of Ambler and Greene, and would be a paranoid fantasy anywhere but Los Angeles, where it is simply naturalistic social fiction as cool as John O'Hara at his iciest.

But Ambler and Greene are, compared to Chandler, relatively humorless writers; it was Chandler's genius to treat this mean city with so much grotesque and ironic comedy that he literally created the modern style of Black Humor three decades before Lenny Bruce, Joseph Heller, William S. Burroughs, Kurt Vonnegut, Jr., or whoever wrote *Illuminatus!*

As Chandler once wrote in the *Atlantic Monthly*, "Murder, which is a frustration of the individual and hence a frustration of the race, may have, and in fact has, a good deal of sociological implications." Which is only to say that there are reasons, which most of us would prefer not to know, why America has one murder every fourteen minutes and the Swedes hardly ever have a violent assault. Digging out these reasons, the frustrations of our culture as exemplified and heightened by the sun-belt hedonism of Los Angeles, is what Chandler's mysteries are about. His contempt for the puzzle type of detective story was based on the fact that it was *only* a puzzle, and didn't face these implications; as he said, the authors preferred to forget "that murder is an act of infinite cruelty."

Chandler added, hinting at the function of humor in his work, "It is not funny that a man should be killed, but it is sometimes funny that he should be killed for so little, and that his death should be the coin of what we call civilization." When you have finally untangled the plot of *The Little Sister* (another deceptively sedate Chandler title for a blood-spattered horror story), the hidden conspiracy goes back to a large studio's attempt to protect the reputation of a rising actress, and to the decisions of a producer so eccentric he allows his dogs to pee in his office even though it disgusts his secretaries. He *can* allow his dogs to pee in the office, or anywhere, because he has the money and power to do whatever the hell he wants. This is satire, yes, but it is deadly accurate. See the career of Howard Hughes.

It is commonplace to say that the humor of Chandler's brutal stories lies in the fa-

Haiku by Raymond Chandler

Police Woman
To say her face would stop a clock
    would be to insult her.
It would stop a runaway horse.

Actress
She smelled the way
    the Taj Mahal looks
    by moonlight.

Silent Intruder
A wedge of sunlight
    slipped over the edge of the desk
and fell noiselessly on the carpet.

Pathos
Her voice faded off into a sort of sad
whisper
    like a mortician
    asking for a down payment.

Los Angeles
One great big
    sun-tanned
        hangover.

Seascape
On the right the great fat solid Pacific
    trudging into shore
like a scrubwoman going home.

Another Lady
She had a mouth
    that seemed made
for three-decker sandwiches.

Malibu
More wind-blown hair and sunglasses
    and attitudes
    and pseudorefined voices
        and waterfront morals.

Finale
I never saw any of them again
    —except the cops.
No way has yet been invented to say
    goodbye to them.

mous Chandler style. But that style is not merely comic; it is capable of haiku-like beauty, and at its best it can say literally *anything*. For instance, the emotional impact of Chandler's books lies in something that critics have not widely discussed: his capacity to render physiological sensations (neurological nuances) which most writers have avoided as being totally beyond words. Somehow, Chandler found the words—for the stages of hallucination and pain through which Marlowe rises gradually to consciousness after being beaten senseless, for the ghastly quiet in a room after you have found a dead body, for drug trips that even the psychedelic writers of the '60s have not rendered so precisely, for the intolerable boredom and sudden moments of terror that make up an investigator's life. American English, as it is called—that is a euphemism for underworld and show-biz slang—joins with classic Engligh English, in Chandler's style, to form the most genuine synthesis of Folk Art and High Art we have seen in this country.

It is an axiom of *bon-ton* literary criticism that the style should fit the subject; Chandler meets that standard with such ease he hardly seems to be trying. When he describes Los Angeles as "a big department store of a city with no more personality than a paper cup," he is precise the way Ezra Pound is precise. The department store is the *mot juste* for both the commercialism and the startling juxtapositions of L.A.; the paper cup is an emblem of mass production and quick obsolescence that no Imagist poet could improve. If people are being stabbed, shot, beaten, framed, and betrayed all over the landscape, a style based on deliberate semantic miscegenation (humor in the wrong place, beauty when you least expect it, the continuous shock of jumping from slums to mansions, from dirty police interrogation rooms to jacaranda trees blooming in Laurel Canyon) is a montage of Paradise Lost, a world that could be unspeakably beautiful if power were not being so relentlessly abused everywhere in it.

"In everything that can be called art there is a quality of redemption," Chandler once wrote. This appears in his novels through the personal honor of the hero, Philip Marlowe, but it is only moving and convincing and exemplary because Chandler himself believed it and lived it. The most revealing story in MacShane's biography concerns Chandler's outrage when a Paramount executive offered him a $5,000 bonus to finish a script on time. Since Chandler had contracted to finish the script on time, the bonus appeared an insult to him—an honorable man lives up to a contract signed—and he indignantly refused it. This exactly parallels the instances in which Marlowe refuses or returns a client's fee, because he has failed to do an adequate job—scenes that probably seem incredible to the average reader in this cynical and swinish decade. Such scenes of old-fashioned morality remain powerful because they were written with the one ingredient no writer can fake: total sincerity.

What Chandler added to the detective story was not just style and humor and sociological depth; he added his own sense of the mysterious psychology of courage—something nobody can ever totally own or totally lose. The eighth or ninth layer of humor in his books, when you've read them as often as I have, lies in Marlowe's acute awareness that his courage just possibly might not be there when he needs it. To know that we live in a world where murder is the "coin of civilization" is to live on the edge of nothing, like the Existentialist; to build a philosophy of courage in the teeth of that high sense of vulnerability is to live with a romantic myth that might collapse abruptly, like Hemingway, who died a suicide; to believe in courage, and in honor, and in even more old-fashioned virtues, while acknowledging that courage itself might leave you as rudely as a Hollywood agent slams his door on a fading star, is to live in the Black Comedy that Chandler captured better than any other novelist of our century.

A 1950s poll found that only two artists were equally popular with highbrows and lowbrows. One was, of course, Marilyn Monroe. The other was, deservedly, Raymond Chandler. His novels are all still in print even though the earliest of them is set in the 1930s and the last in the early 1950s and they seem superficially "dated." They are as topical as the latest theory about the Cowboy and Yankee war among conspiracy buffs. We are still in the world Chandler

described, and he has much to teach us about how to laugh and remain honorable and decent in such a world.

EPICENE WILDEBLOOD is the most highly esteemed literary critic in the United States. He has never been known to split an infinitive or to descend to pleonasm. Due to circumstances beyond his control he has appeared in four vulgar, common science-fiction novels, where he was not treated gently, and he is still engaged in trying to find his way back to the Real World. "I am not a character in fiction," he insists, "but a critic of fiction. The difference should be clear to anyone with a sound mind. Don't you believe me? Please say you believe me...."

Reprinted by permission of *City Miner Magazine.* P.O. Box 176, Berkeley, CA 94701. Subscriptions $4/year.

Courage is something you can never totally own or totally lose.

Item

The Riddle Song

by Robin Marion

Who is she that sang so fair
Brought such sweetness to the air?
Who is she
O who is she
That laughed among the flowers
For two eternal hours?
Who is she
O who is she
With skirt of moss and hair of leaves?
Who but my lady Greensleeves?

Who is she
Say, who is she
With eye so bold and smile so free?
Great mother of God
Say, who is she?
To bring such bliss
With her fairy kiss
To medicine each heart that grieves?
Who but my lady Greensleeves?

ROBIN MARION is the leader of a group of bisexual witches who haunt the woods of Mendocino, Sonoma, and Marin.

JOHN DILLINGER CABAL, POSITION PAPER 23

Stupidynamics

by Simon Moon

E volutionary perspective suggests the following propositions may be true or may serve as plausible working principles until we understand the brain better.

1. Stupidity is partly genetic and partly acquired.
2. The genetic portion of stupidity is programmed into all of us and consists of "typical mammalian behavior." That is, a

A great deal of the human nervous system is on autopilot, like the chimpanzee nervous system.

great deal of the human nervous system is on autopilot, like the closely related chimpanzee nervous system and the more distantly related cow nervous system. The programs of territoriality, pack hierarchy, etc., are evolutionarily stable strategies and hence work *mechanically*, without conscious thought. These evolutionary relative successes became genetic programs because

132

they work well enough for the ordinary mammal in ordinary mammalian affairs. They only become stupidities in human beings, where the higher cortical centers have been developed as *a monitoring system to feed back more sophisticated survival techniques and correct these stereotyped programs with more flexible ones.*

In short, to the extent that a human follows the genetic primate-pack patterns, without feedback from the cortex, that human is still acting like an ape, and hasn't acquired facility in using the New Brain.

3. The acquired portion of stupidity is the result of enculturation, which is the process by which the flexible, multivalued human nervous system is brainwashed into surrendering its flexibility and repeating (miming) the stereotyped behaviors, beliefs, values, etc., of the tribe into which it is born.

4. *Primate behavior only changes under the impact of new technology.* A band of chimpanzees will repeat, robotically, the same behaviors over millenniums or longer; if somebody teaches them how to use sticks to obtain food, or a simple sign language, they will immediately change their behavior under the "shock" of this new technology. Human societies (e.g., China, Byzantium) can also remain static and repetitious for long times, until new technology triggers new behaviors.

5. Domesticated primates (humans) have changed more in the past hundred years than in all previous history, under the impact of an *accelerated acceleration* of new technologies. The Wright Brothers, Edison, Einstein, Ford, etc., have triggered more behavior change than all the political revolutionaries, Right or Left, of this century.

6. From points 3, 4, and 5, it follows that the quickest way to change primate behavior is to introduce a new technology, and

that technology is the strongest medicine that can be administered to cure stupidity or at least to alleviate it somewhat.

7. Genetic behavior changes more rapidly than acquired behavior when new technology is introduced, because the genetic code

---

Primate behavior only changes under the impact of new technology.

---

contains what Lorenz calls "holes," or *points of imprint vulnerability*, where new imprints (networks of new neurogenetic circuits) can be formed. Shock and confusion, two side-products of new technology, trigger this sort of imprint vulnerability.*

8. High intelligence is the ability to receive, integrate, and transmit new signals rapidly. (This follows from Wiener's *Cybernetics*, especially his classic definition, "To live effectively is to live with adequate information," and from Shannon's *Mathematical Theory of Communication*.)

9. Stupidity is a blockage in the ability to receive, integrate, and transmit new signals rapidly. Genetic programs, if uncorrected by new imprints, can cause such signal-blindness: genetic behavior is mechanical, "unconscious," uncorrected by the subtle feedback circuits of the higher nervous centers. Enculturation (identifying the tribal reality map with "reality") can also cause signal-blindness: signals not consistent with the tribal mythology are repressed,

---

* For further information on the role of shock in forming new imprints, see Timothy Leary, *Exo-Psychology*. For further information on the role of confusion, see Paul Watzlawick, *How Real Is Real?*

133

ignored, covered over with projections or distortions until they do fit the local mythos, or are simply "forgotten" very quickly.

Stupidity is a blockage in the ability to receive, integrate, and transmit new signals.

10. Domesticated primates, like wild primates, want chiefly an *alpha male* to lead them. The more closely this figure approximates the primordial archetype—i.e., the meanest-tempered baboon in the herd—the more fervently the other primates will follow him. (This explains the otherwise inexplicable elevation to power of distinctly subhuman types, e.g., Mussolini, Nixon, Hitler, Stalin. The primate logic is "If he's that *baaaaaaaad*"—in the sense in which baaaaaaaad is used in Black ghetto argot—"he'll scare hell out of competing primate bands.")

11. After finding an alpha male to lead them, domesticated primates then seek a scapegoat on whom to blame their troubles. They do so because solving problems requires intelligence, and there is still more stupidity than intelligence on this planet. Domesticated primates are not optimistic about solving their problems, which seem hopeless in their confused state, midway between mammalian reflexes and objective consciousness. It is easier, to a stupid mind, to find somebody else to blame for the problems.

12. The chief function of the alpha male in a domesticated primate pack is to find, denounce, and lead the persecution of such scapegoats, internal and external.

13. To wild primates, as to other mammals, emotions function as emergency signals, mobilizing energy for "threat" situations, i.e., challenges to territoriality or to status in the pack hierarchy.

14. To domesticated primates, emotions serve both of the above functions, but also serve two new functions made possible by the new brain and its symbolizing capacities. These new functions are (1) to stave off boredom and (2) to gain status or power.

15. Wild primates, like other mammals, have no defense against boredom. They simply go to sleep when nothing exciting is happening. (This is also an evolutionarily stable strategy, since it keeps them out of trouble. You are less visible to a predator when still than when moving; you are less likely to get your nose or your paws into a beehive, etc.) Domesticated primates learn, by mimicry of their elders, a skill that has been passed on among hominids for millenniums: how to use emotions to stave off this existential boredom.

Domesticated primates are not optimistic about solving their problems. It is easier to blame somebody.

16. The only other way to stave off boredom, in a complex domesticated primate like humankind, is to increase one's consciousness and intelligence. This is not appealing to the average primate, who instead invents emotional games (soap-opera and grand-opera dramatics) to keep life exciting. The writings of Eric Berne and

134

the Transactional Analysts are mostly concerned with cataloging these emotional games, or cons.

Emotional games (soap-opera and grand-opera dramatics) keep life exciting.

---

17. Among domesticated primates, emotions also confer status and power. That is, the most emotional person in the room "dominates" everyone else in the room: they must all react to his or her emotions, one way or another, or surrender the turf by retreating from the room entirely.

18. Almost all children begin to learn some of these stereotyped emotional games or cons from parents and siblings by about the age of two. They then experiment with these power tactics (mammalian politics) until they have learned how to score points (symbolic victories) by means of emotional blackmail.

19. Very few children ever learn, from parents, teachers, or anybody else, the techniques of rational problem-solving.

20. From 18 and 19, it follows that, on this primitive planet, most people will try to handle their problems symbolically, by emotional game-playing, and relatively few will know how to solve their problems rationally.

21. Stupidity, being partly genetic, partly acquired by enculturation, and partly the result of mimicry of emotional status games, is highly contagious. The stupidest party in any situation drags all the others down to his or her level. Trying to reason with an emotional person is frustrating,

because useless; the only way to "deal" with them, except by escaping the scene, is to challenge their emotional game with a strong counter-game.

22. Since primate behavior can be changed by new technology, the only cure for the stupidity of the human species must be a technology that itself immediately and permanently increases intelligence.

23. Such an intelligence-raising technology must be hedonic; i.e., it must offer greater pleasure to the users, or it will not come into wide use very rapidly.

24. When such a hedonic intelligence-raising device is invented, the rulers of society will attempt to repress it as a threat to stability.

(24a. If such a hedonic intelligence-raising device has been invented, it will have been repressed. Researchers will have been imprisoned or intimidated; distributors will have been pursued more vigorously than murderers or thieves; the device itself will be pictured as terrible and dangerous in all the mass media.)

25. Until the existence of such a hedonic intelligence-raiser is unambiguously proven, certain steps can be taken to decrease stupidity slightly.

26. *Biosurvival stupidity* is imprinted almost immediately after birth, is caused by traumatic fright (due to our primitive child-rearing practices), and takes the form of chronic anxiety. This is epidemic in our society; a 1968 US Public Health survey showed that 85 per cent of the population have some symptom of chronic anxiety, e.g., heart palpitations, frequent nightmares, dizzy spells, etc. Chronic depression usually accompanies this. In the extreme forms, one finds autism or catatonia, which are biopsychic or cellular "decisions" that human beings are just too nasty to be worth relating to, or paranoia, the fine art of

finding enemies everywhere, especially among one's friends.

27. Biosurvival stupidity causes so much stress on the organism, and so much alienation from other humans, that it creates stupidity on all the other neural circuits as well, and thereby prevents the development of a high level of intelligence on *any* circuit.

28. Biosurvival stupidity can be alleviated by the practice of various martial arts (akido, karate, kung fu, etc.); by *asana*, the yogic technique of holding one posture for long periods of time every day; or by psychotherapy. Asana and psychotherapy take much longer to produce dramatic effects than martial arts do, but may be necessary in acute cases.

Biosurvival stupidity can be alleviated by martial arts.

29. *Emotional stupidity* is imprinted when the toddler is first learning "family politics" (mammalian hierarchy games). Typically, the victim confronts all problematic situations in interpersonal relations with one stereotyped emotional game (e.g., a good long sulk, a temper tantrum, "depression," a drunken bender, suicide threats, howling or blustering in traditional angry-primate manner, etc). One or another of these robotic emotional reflexes can be found in about 99 per cent of the population.

30. Emotional stupidity can be alleviated by the yogic breathing technique known as *pranayama*, or by the Gurdjieff techniques of establishing an internal "Observer" who monitors the emotional reflexes, i.e., makes

them *conscious* instead of *mechanical*. Pranayama produces quicker results; the Gurdjieff techniques ultimately produce deeper, more long-lasting results.

Emotional stupidity can be alleviated by pranayama.

31. *Semantic stupidity* is imprinted when the older child begins dealing with words and concepts (abstract artifacts produced by the higher brain centers after the human stock separated out from the other primates). The most pervasive form of semantic stupidity consists of confusing the local (tribal) reality map with the all of reality. Dogmatism, rigid ideological systems, and bizarre reality maps (ideational schizophrenias) are also rampant. Symbol-blindness, ranging from verbal illiteracy to mathematical or artistic illiteracy, is also common, and often found in those who are very skillful in handling one narrow range of symbols; e.g., the painter who can't solve a quadratic equation, the scientist who can't or won't read poetry, etc.

32. Semantic stupidity can be alleviated by a diet rich in lecithin and protein, by courses in remedial reading, logic, and scientific method, and by practice in General Semantics.

33. *Sociosexual stupidity* is imprinted when the DNA blueprint triggers the mutation to puberty. It consists of robotic repetition of one stereotyped sex-role, usually accompanied by a deep-seated conviction that all other sex-roles are abnormal ("mad" or "bad").

34. The only alleviations for sociosexual

stupidity currently available are the various forms of psychotherapy, of which Group Encounter is probably most effective.

35. Alleviating or totally curing these four types of stupidity would produce human beings roughly matching the idealistic definition given by Robert Heinlein in *Time Enough For Love*:

"A human being should be able to change a diaper, plan an invasion, butcher a hog, design a building, conn a ship, write a sonnet, balance accounts, build a wall, set a bone, comfort the dying, take orders, give orders, cooperate, act alone, solve equations, analyze a new problem, pitch manure, program a computer, cook a tasty meal, fight efficiently, die gallantly."

36. Roughly speaking, if you can handle 14 out of Heinlein's 21 programs, you have released ⅔ of your potential intelligence, and are ⅔ of a human being. If you can handle seven of them, you are ⅓ of a human being. Scores above 14 mean you're prob-

ably a genius and probably know it; scores below 7 mean you're certainly a moron, and certainly don't know it (i.e., you are convinced, are you not, that the world is really a terrible place and that your inability to cope is due to the world's evil rather than to your own stupidity?).

If the world seems to be getting nastier, your stupidity is increasing.

37. A quicker intelligence test, which also indicates the trajectory of your development, is this:

If the world seems to be getting bigger and funnier all the time, your intelligence is steadily increasing.

If the world seems to be getting smaller and nastier all the time, your stupidity is steadily increasing.

Paleopuritanism and Neopuritanism

by Marvin Gardens

S piro Agnew, like great Babylon in St. John's *Revelation*, has fallen, has fallen! But the seeds he planted—little tiny Spirochetes, so to speak—have bloomed everywhere, and a new age of irrationalism is upon us. In particular, a new, improved strain of the old Puritan virus is loose in the land, represented on the right hand by Nixon's Supreme Court and on the left hand by the fascisto-feminist wing of Women's Liberation.

To a libertarian there is one rule in love as in all life: non-invasiveness. Do not enter somebody's physical or mental "space" unless invited. This is rooted in ethology, in the biological basis of animal life, and was defined, in purely logical terms even before ethology emerged as a science, by Benjamin Tucker. The rule of non-invasiveness, also stated by Warren as "Mind Your Own Business," means, when applied to sex, that when people make sexual overtures to you, you have a perfect right to say "Yes!" or "No!" as bluntly as necessary and without too excessive a worry about hurting their feelings or damaging their precious egos. They have entered your territory, and it is for you to decide whether to welcome them or chase them out. However, whatever they are doing without your participation, whether it be coupling in twos or in threes or in Mongolian clusters; whether it be hetero or homo or involves German shepherds, is none of your business, and you scarcely have the right to hold an opinion about it. Or, if you must have an opinion, you still owe them a decent respect for their privacy and should offer your words as a suggestion, not as a Divine Commandment.

This is simple and straightforward, and, even before the invention of libertarian ideology, has generally been accepted by highly educated men and women in all civilizations, although it clearly goes against the grain of most major religions.

Puritanism takes the opposite position, and Mencken was quite accurate in defining it as "the haunting fear that somebody, somewhere, might be having a good time." The Puritan feels that what other people are doing in the privacy of their boudoirs, even if it doesn't affect him physically, is of paramount importance and must be supervised and policed. Some health-food crusaders steer quite close to oral Puritanism in their obsession that everybody else eat the "right" diet.

The old, right-wing Puritanism generally favored heterosexuality, within legal (and, preferably, religious) monogamy. The new, left-wing Puritanism generally favors homosexuality or masturbation and regards heterosex as the Devil's Workshop. The emotional tone and the desire to butt into other people's private lives is the same in both cases; both are fascistoid and anti-libertarian.

Puritanism invades libertarian groups via the old Marxists (who were always Puritans) and the new feminists (who are not always Puritans). The key was the word "sexism," which originally had a specific meaning akin to "racism." That is, just as racism consists of a stereotyped negative response to a whole class of human beings selected by racial characteristics, sexism denoted, originally, a stereotyped negative response to another whole class of human beings selected by sexual characteristics. Words, however, do not often retain one simple meaning, as the semanticists know, and "sexism" soon acquired a penumbra of secondary and irrelevant associations. Pornography became "sexist," erotica became "sexist," and eventually, freedom itself became "sexist."

For perfect precision, let me include here an attempted neurosemantic analysis of the Puritan reflexes. Although this analysis is technical, it is also, I hope, free of the ambiguities of most polemic on this subject.

The old, conservative Puritanism and the new, radical Puritanism are both based on phobic imprinting of the second neurological circuit (the motion-emotion circuit), together with identification reflexes in the third (semantic) circuit and further phobic imprinting of the fourth (sociosexual) circuit.

To quote Leary,

"Phylogenetically the second neural circuit evolved in the early Palaeozoic period (500 million years B.C.), when the first vertebrates and amphibians began to rise up against and free themselves from the pull of gravity. The ability to dominate, locomote, and exert superior force became a survival asset. The emotional circuit of man's nervous system is thus an emergency device. When the human being acts in an emotional way, he or she is reverting to a most primitive phase of brute rage or terror."

Both the Old Puritanism and the New Puritanism are forms of emotional plague.

Basic emotions are imprinted upon the second circuit during the crawling and toddling stages of infancy. Puritanism is imprinted when the child is taught aversive, loathing, shameful reflexes toward its own anal-genital parts. The parental figures first exhibit these reactions themselves, then withdraw love when the infant fails to exhibit the same reactions, then reward (reinforce) the infant for learning to exhibit these reactions. Permanent emotions of shame and guilt are thus imprinted, with considerable blurring of anal and genital distinctions.

These emotions, being largely glandular, function mechanically, as Gurdjieff emphasized. There is no so-called "free will," "autonomy," or "human dignity" on the emotional level. As Leary says so precisely, "Emotions are the lowest form of consciousness.... Emotions are caused by biochemical secretions in the body to serve during the state of acute emergency. An emotional person is a blind, crazed maniac." Imprinted phobic emotions are the cause of that state of "chronic low-grade emergency" epidemic in our culture, according to Perls, Hefferline, Goodman (*Gestalt Therapy*). The phobic person enters each situation with the emergency reflexes already turned on.

There is no free will or human dignity on the emotional level.

The imprinting of the third, semantic circuit occurs when the child begins handling and questioning. This circuit "mediates fine, precise muscular activities, especially speech" (Leary). Depending on parental imprinting techniques, the child can learn to handle and question freely or to be clumsy, stupid, timid, fearful, etc. Usually, the imprint encourages dexterity and fluency in some areas and total taboo in others.

The blurring of anal and genital, characteristic of Puritanism, is here reinforced by parental vocabulary. The key words applying anal imagery to the genitalia are "dirty," "filthy," "barnyard morals," "open sewer of pornography," "pig," "animal," etc. "Smut," from Old English *smotten*, to blacken or stain, *cf.* smudge, acts to generalize the anal phobia beyond sex to anything dark, including black humans, who are often irrationally feared or hated by both the old Puritans and the new Puritans.

The anality of the old Puritans was generally low-profile and "buried in the language," through the constant dirt metaphor associated with genitality, or in such expressions as "Don't be piggy, Johnny." The new Puritans represent an unconscious irruption of these elements. Their favorite

word is "shit," which can appear as often as twice or more in each sentence. Jokes, of a childish nature, about flatulence are omnipresent and compulsive in their writings. The "pig" archetype is everywhere. When they rise above this infantile semantics, on occasion, it is only to the adolescent level of compulsive masturbation metaphor.

Thus, the Puritan personality starts from aversive emotional imprints, which are then complicated by a special reinforcing vocabulary associating all sexuality with the anal shit-dirt-mess aversion reflexes. The semantic imprint functions in harmony with the emotional-glandular imprint.

The fourth, sociosexual circuit is then imprinted with a "Mr. District Attorney" or "Holy Inquisitor" persona. Stimuli in the external world which trigger the anal guilt-shame reflexes in the Puritan are mediated through the semantic circuit, where the "smut" or "sexism" or whatever label is affixed, and the emotion is discharged by attacking the person who was the source of the stimuli.

The Pig Archetype is everywhere: "Don't be piggy, Johnny!"

As Korzybski points out in *Science and Sanity*, this habitual confusion between internal evaluation and external stimuli is a neurosemantic habit acquired from traditional education. In general semantics, this habit is called "identification." It is comparable to the conditioned reflexes observed by Behaviorists in animal studies; although normal for animals, it is abnormal for humans. It short-circuits the higher, cortical functions, and leaves the person operating on thalamic circuits only, thereby preventing the characteristically human functions of reason, science, creativity, invention, etc.

IDENTIFICATION IS THUS A MILD FORM OF HALLUCINATION. Those who identify their own imprinted emotional-glandular response with the external stimuli, for instance, cannot imagine how the stimuli appear to someone else who has not had their imprinting. In Korzybski's metaphor, they act as if the map is the territory (or as Alan Watts says, they act as if the menu is the meal). Their own emotions are all that is real to them, in a taboo area covered by phobic imprint, and they have never experienced any stimuli in that area without anxiety, in a neutral or objective way.

As psychologist Theodore Schroeder pointed out, "obscenity" is the modern form of "black magic." Both concepts are operationally meaningless; there is no instrument which, pointed at a book or painting, will tell how much "black magic" or "obscenity" is in it. These things are in the nervous system of the observer, imprinted in the manner described above. Attributing them to books, art, ideas, etc., in the external world, and seeking to punish the perpetrators, is the same kind of hallucination that produced the witch-hunts in which nine million innocents were killed.

Clarification of this issue explains what the Buddhists mean by "maya." One could lead a group of both old Puritans and new Puritans through a gallery featuring photographs of flowers without any problem arising, even though flowers are the genitals of plants, as everyone who passed Botany 101 knows. However, try to navigate that group through an exhibit of photos of animal geni-

talia and almost anything could happen, when the emotional imprints are activated. The external stimuli (natural sexuality) are the same, but the imprints are different. Contemplation of this parable should clarify what Buddha meant in saying that most people see only their own "maya" and never experience objective fact at all. Of course, if the exhibit featured human genitalia, the fourth and third circuits would be activated, and a great deal of angry speech about "smut" from the first group and "sexism" from the second would be heard. All of this speech would confuse the internal glandular-emotional emergency imprint with the objective external stimuli, and there would be a desire to punish the photographer.

Emotional Identification is a mild form of hallucination.

This confusion of map with territory cannot be removed by argument or even conditioning, since it rests upon imprinting. Any attempt to discuss the problem rationally leads, inevitably, sooner or later, to some of the taboo words, phrases, associations, etc., which trigger the emergency reflexes again, and the rage reflexes, as always, follow swiftly. It is even dangerous to defend any person chosen as a target for the punishing discharge of the Puritans' fear-rage secretions. The defender becomes the next target, as in the witch-hunts of the past.

Reich distinguished between neurosis, which is painful only to the carrier, and emotional plague, which is dangerous to

141

anyone living in the same society with the carrier. In this sense, both conservative old Puritanism and radical new Puritanism are emotional plague, and the carriers are neurosemantic Typhoid Marys. No amount of sympathy for the carriers should blind us to the fact of their social role. Dr. Wilhelm Reich and Dr. Timothy Leary, the only scientists to dare to confront this problem directly, were railroaded into prison, not in Nazi Germany or Soviet Russia, but in the allegedly secular, supposedly scientific United States. "An emotional person is a blind, crazed maniac," and the new Puritans, having an ideology which justifies them in indulging emotion and in refusing to attempt even an effort at reasonableness or fairness, are probably more dangerous than the old.

As soon as this analysis is understood, it should be, as far as possible, forgotten. The only way to deal with the new Puritans is the same way the libertarian deals with all human beings: non-invasively, rationally. One must act always as if the other party is a free, rational mind and never get dragged into their own childish and hysterical milieu. If they state that your position is pissy, shitty, and piggy, ignore that. Do not fall into replying in kind by stating that

THEIR position is pissy, shitty, and piggy. Explain the libertarian position logically and clearly, as if you were dealing with rational adults. This will, in the long run, perform the one moral form of segregation: drawing all judicious observers onto one side of the issue and all the fools onto the other.

MARVIN GARDENS is the author of two best-selling novels (Vlad the Barbarian, Vlad Victorious*) and is the founder and chairman of the Linda Lovelace for President Committee. He is currently at work on a non-fiction book which, he says, "will demonstrate, beyond all possibility of doubt, that extraterrestrials have been among us since at least 1965 and have taken over control of publishing and all the mass media, which they are using to defame and discredit the traditional heroic image of mankind in all great art and literature, replacing it with mindrot and semantic black magic that will soften our moral fibres and make us easy prey to conquest, and they are furthermore plotting to slander me as a paranoid so nobody will take my warnings seriously. And they're cutting the cocaine with* Clorox, too."

Item

Art is Technology: Technology is Art

The World's Greatest Intuitive Artist

The World's Greatest Sound Engineer

Art consists of those sciences and technologies that are self-justifying, that delight the apprehension of the beholder.

Science and technology consist of those arts that allow us to understand and alter our circumstances.

Stravinsky was quite correct in calling himself a sound engineer; Jacob Bronowski was equally justified in calling Newton and Einstein great artists. There are demarcations; but there are also overlaps.

The criteria for judging art can only be subjective or statistical. One can say subjectively that the artwork delights oneself, or one can say statistically that it delights x per cent of the population. Saying anything beyond this is the piffle and humbug of professional critics justifying their jobs.

The criteria for judging science and technology are objective and sometimes also statistical. One can say that certain sciences have objectively enhanced life, and that others have been a blight and a pestilence; and one can estimate the percentage of objective benefit or objective harm in a given technology at a given time.

Artists who cannot speak science are partially illiterate; scientists who cannot speak art are partially illiterate.

Item

Nine Million Dead

by Simon Moon

Nine million dead witches are in the room
   with me.
They come tumbling out of the books of
   White
And Murray, Gardner and Taylor, Lea and
   Lecky:
Nine million dead.

One with dark eyelids, a girl not twenty,
One with eyes that flash and laugh like a
   wolf's,
One with a humped back, in rags and sores,
One with a royal crown and a moon-white
   throat:
Nine million dead.

They smell of the dead (a rich, loamy
   smell);
Their eyes are inhuman but wise as a toad's;
They make no sound when they tread on
   the floor:
Nine million dead.

Like a fiddle's trill or the squeak of a bat
Impregnates the air with its own pulsation,
A vibration of fear is in this room
And looks at me with the mad wise eyes
Of nine million dead.

A lipless mouth with teeth all fanged,
Eyeless sockets and a leper's nose,
Long red hair like a crown of glory:
"I am life-in-death and death-in-life:
Kiss my mouth and understand!"
She was the only corpse among
Nine million dead.

Beauty and the Beast at the Empire State,
The Flying Dutchman and the youngest
   son—
It's an old story and it still sings true.
The stone rejected is the cornerstone.
I kissed her once and, through her, kissed
Nine million dead.

She was a nun and a whore, a mother, a
   child,
A snake and a dove and a corpse and a seed,
A boy I loved once and a man I feared
(She was my fear and the cause of my fear).
She was Father and Son and Holy Devil
And nine million dead.

My brain has nova'd and burned to ash,
The universe stripped to its naked skin.
We laughed at the living who could not
   know
The life beyond life and the joy beyond joy,
We nine million dead.

144

The
RICH
Economy

by Mordecai the Foul,
High Priest, Head Temple,
Bavarian Illuminati

I f there is one proposition which currently wins the assent of nearly everybody, it is that we need more jobs. "A cure for unemployment" is promised, or earnestly sought, by every Heavy Thinker from Jimmy Carter to the Communist Party USA, from Ronald Reagan to the head of the economics department at the local university, from the Birchers to the New Left.

I would like to challenge that idea. I don't think there is, or ever again can be, a *cure* for unemployment. I propose that *unemployment is not a disease*, but the natural, healthy functioning of an advanced technological society.

The inevitable direction of any technology, and of any rational species such as *Homo Sap.*, is toward what Buckminster Fuller calls ephemeralization, or doing-more-with-less. For instance, a modern computer does more (handles more bits of information) with less hardware than the proto-computers of the late '40s and '50s. One worker with a modern teletype machine does more in an hour than a thousand medieval monks painstakingly copying scrolls for a century. Atomic fission does more with a cubic centimeter of matter than all the engineers of the 19th century could do with a million tons, and fusion does even more.

Unemployment is not a disease; so it has no "cure."

This tendency toward ephemeralization or doing-more-with-less is based on two principal factors, *viz*:

1. The increment-of-association, a term coined by engineer C. H. Douglas, meaning simply that when we combine our efforts we can do more than the sum of what each of us could do separately. Five people acting synergetically together can lift a small modern car, but if each of the five tries separately, the car will not budge. As society

145

evolved from tiny bands, to larger tribes, to federations of tribes, to city-states, to nations, to multinational alliances, the increment-of-association increased exponentially. A stone-age hunting band could not build the Parthenon; a Renaissance city-state could not put Neil Armstrong on the Moon. When the increment-of-association increases, through larger social units, doing-more-with-less becomes increasingly possible.

2. Knowledge itself is inherently self-augmenting. Every discovery "suggests" further discoveries; every innovation provokes further innovations. This can be seen, concretely, in the records of the US Patent Office, where you will find more patents granted every year than were granted the year before, in a rising curve that seems to be headed toward infinity. If inventor A can make a Whatsit out of 20 moving parts, inventor B will come along and build a Whatsit of 10 moving parts, inventor C of 5 moving parts. If the technology of 1900 can get 100 ergs out of a Whatchamacallum, the technology of 1950 can get 1,000 ergs, 2000 can get 100,000 ergs. Again, the tendency is always toward doing-more-with-less.*

Unemployment is directly caused by this technological capacity to do-more-with-less. Thousands of monks were technologically unemployed by Gutenberg. Thousands of blacksmiths were technologically unemployed by Ford's Model T. Each device that does-more-with-less makes human labor that much less necessary.

Aristotle said that slavery could only be abolished when machines were built that

---

* I cannot spend more space on this point here. Those who want more evidence of the doing-more-with-less phenomenon should consult Fuller's *Operating Manual for Spaceship Earth* and Alfred Korzybski's *Manhood of Humanity*.

could operate themselves. Working for wages, the modern equivalent of slavery — very accurately called "wage slavery" by social critics — is in the process of being abolished by just such self-programming machines. In fact, Norbert Wiener, one of the creators of cybernetics, foresaw this as early as 1947 and warned that we would have massive unemployment once the computer revolution really got moving.

It is arguable, and I for one would argue, that the only reason Wiener's prediction has not totally been realized yet — although we do have ever-increasing unemployment — is that the big unions, the corporations, and government have all tacitly agreed to slow down the pace of cybernation, to drag their feet and run the economy with brakes on. This is because they all, still, regard unemployment as a "disease" and cannot imagine a "cure" for the nearly total unemployment that full cybernation will create.

Suppose, for a moment, we challenge this Calvinistic mind-set. Let us regard wage-work — as most people do, in fact, regard it — as a curse, a drag, a nuisance, a barrier that stands between us and what we really want to do. In that case, your job is the disease, and unemployment is the cure.

"But without working for wages we'll all starve to death!?! Won't we?"

Not at all. Many farseeing social thinkers have suggested intelligent and plausible plans for adapting to a society of rising unemployment. Here are some examples.

1. The National Dividend. This was invented by engineer C. H. Douglas and has been revived with some modifications by poet Ezra Pound and designer Buckminster Fuller. The basic idea (although Douglas, Pound, and Fuller differ on details) is that every citizen should be declared a shareholder in the nation, and should

receive dividends on the Gross National Product for the year. Estimates differ as to how much this would be for each citizen, but at the current level of the GNP it is conservative to say that a share would be worth several times as much, per year, as a welfare recipient receives—at least five times more.

Critics complain that this would be inflationary. Supporters of the National Dividend reply that it would only be inflationary if the dividends distributed were *more than* the GNP; and they are proposing only to issue dividends *equal to* the GNP.

2. The Guaranteed Annual Income. This has been urged by economist Robert Theobald and others. The government would simply establish an income level above the poverty line and guarantee that no citizen would receive less; if your wages fall below that level, or you have no wages, the government makes up the difference.

This plan would definitely cost the government less than the present welfare system, with all its bureaucratic red tape and redundancy: a point worth considering for those conservatives who are always complaining about the high cost of welfare. It would also spare the recipients the humiliation, degradation, and dehumanization built into the present welfare system: a point for liberals to consider. A system that is less expensive than welfare and also less debasing to the poor, it seems to me, should not be objectionable to anybody but hardcore sadists.

3. The Negative Income Tax. This was devised by Nobel economist Milton Friedman and is a less radical variation on the above ideas. The Negative Income Tax would establish a minimum income for every citizen; anyone whose income fell below that level would receive the amount necessary to bring them up to that standard. Friedman, who is sometimes called a conservative but prefers to title himself a libertarian, points out that this would cost "the government" (i.e., the taxpayers) *less than* the present welfare system, like Theobald's Guaranteed Annual Income. It would also dispense with the last tinge of humiliation associated with government "charity," since when you cashed a check from IRS nobody (not even your banker) would know if it was supplementary income due to poverty or a refund due to overpayment of last year's taxes.

4. The RICH Economy. This was devised by inventor L. Wayne Benner (coauthor with Timothy Leary of *Terra II*) in collaboration with the present author. It's a four-stage program to retool society for the cybernetic and space-age future we are rapidly entering. RICH means Rising Income through Cybernetic Homeostasis.

Stage I is to recognize that cybernation and massive unemployment are inevitable *and to encourage them*. This can be done by offering a $100,000 reward to any worker who can design a machine that will replace him or her, and all others doing the same work. In other words, instead of being dragged into the cybernetic age kicking and screaming, we should charge ahead bravely, regarding the Toilless Society as the Utopian goal humanity has always sought.

Stage II is to establish either the Negative Income Tax or the Guaranteed Annual Income, so that the massive unemployment caused by Stage I will not throw hordes of people into the degradation of the present welfare system.

Stage III is to gradually, experimentally, raise the Guaranteed Annual Income to the level of the National Dividend suggested by Douglas, Bucky Fuller, and Ezra Pound, which would give every citizen the approximate living standard of the comfortable middle class. The reason for doing this gradually is to pacify those conservative economists who claim that the National Dividend is "inflationary" or would practically wreck the banking business by lowering the interest rate to near-zero. It is our claim that this would not happen as long as the total dividends distributed to the populace equaled the Gross National Product. But since this is a revolutionary and controversial idea, it would be prudent, we allow, to approach it in slow steps, raising the minimum income perhaps 5 per cent per year for the first ten years. And, *after the massive cybernation caused by Stage I has produced a glut of consumer goods,* experimentally raise it further and faster toward the level of a true National Dividend.

Stage IV is a massive investment in adult education, for two reasons. (1) People can spend only so much time fucking, smoking dope, and watching TV; after a while they get bored. This is the main psychological objection to the workless society, and the answer to it is to educate people for functions more cerebral than fucking, smoking dope, watching TV, or the idiot jobs most are currently toiling at. (2) There are vast challenges and opportunities confronting us in the next three or four decades, of which the most notable are those highlighted in Tim Leary's SMI²LE slogan— Space Migration, Intelligence Increase, Life Extension. Humanity is about to enter an entirely new evolutionary relationship to space, time, and consciousness. We will no longer be limited to one planet, to a brief, less-than-a-century lifespan, and to the stereotyped and robotic mental processes by which most people currently govern their lives. Everybody deserves the chance, if they want it, to participate in the evolutionary leap to what Leary calls "more space, more time, and more intelligence to

enjoy space and time."

What I am proposing, in brief, is that the Work Ethic (find a Master to employ you for wages, or live in squalid poverty) is obsolete. A Work Esthetic will have to arise to replace this old Stone Age syndrome of the slave, the peasant, the serf, the prole, the wage-worker—the human labor-machine who is not fully a person but, as Marx said, "a tool, an automaton." Delivered from the role of things and robots, people will learn to become fully developed persons, in the sense of the Human Potential movement. They will not seek work out of economic necessity, but out of psychological necessity—as an outlet for their creative potential.

("Creative potential" is not a panchreston. It refers to the inborn drive to play, to tinker, to explore, and to experiment, shown by every child before his or her mental processes are stunted by authoritarian education and operant-conditioned wage-robotry.)

As Bucky Fuller says, the first thought of people, once they are delivered from wage-slavery, will be, "What was it that I was so interested in as a youth, before I was told I had to earn a living?" The answer to that question, coming from millions and then billions of persons liberated from mechanical toil, will make the Renaissance look like a high school science fair or a Greenwich Village art show.

Reprinted by permission of *City Miner Magazine.* P.O. Box 176, Berkeley, CA 94701. Subscriptions $4/year.

Dissociation of Ideas, 5

Distinguish between wealth, illth, and money.

Wealth is best conceived as all the changes in the "natural" (prehuman) environment that are to the benefit of humanity and/or other life forms. A bridge that gets you across the river without your having to stop and build a raft is wealth in this sense. So is an airport. So is the furniture in your house. Think of ten other examples.

Illth, a term coined by John Ruskin, can be conceived as all the changes in the environment that are detrimental to humanity and/or to life itself. Weaponry, then, should be classed as illth, not wealth. Think of ten other examples.

Money is neither wealth nor illth but merely tickets for the transfer of wealth or illth.

Proof: if all the money disappeared overnight, the national standard of living would not change (whatever happened to individuals in the interim); things would be back to normal as soon as the Treasury printed more tickets. But if all the real wealth and illth — all the industrial plant, natural resources, roads, communications, and "real capital" generally — were to disappear, we would be plunged back into the Stone Ages and no issue of currency would improve the situation.

Note also that for all the "real capital" to disappear, all the technical knowhow in human heads would have to vanish. No economist, to my knowledge, has tried to calculate how much of our "real capital" consists of ideas in human heads (brain power) and/or of canned ideas stored in libraries or on tape. A reasonable guess is that 90 per cent of our wealth and illth consists of such.brain creations.

149

About the Author

Visionary, humorist, novelist, playwright, poet, popular science writer, libertarian philosopher, adept—Robert Anton Wilson is a man of many parts.

One of the founders of the Institute for the Study of Human Future, Robert Anton Wilson is also a director of the Prometheus Society, a Maryland-based lobby group engaged in promoting the scientific search for immortality. An active member of the L-5 Society, a group of scientists who are determined to send out the first space-city, Dr. Wilson is vitally concerned with humanity's new frontier.

A former editor at *Playboy* magazine and author of fourteen books, his novel *Illuminatus!* was adapted as a 10-hour science-fiction rock epic and performed under the patronage of Her Majesty Queen Elizabeth II at Great Britain's National Theatre, where Dr. Wilson appeared briefly on stage in a special cameo role.

Illuminatus! has also been performed on the stage in the U.S., Germany, and the Netherlands. Dr. Wilson's works have been published in Sweden, France, Germany, Switzerland, Japan, and throughout the English-speaking world.

Robert Anton Wilson holds a Ph.D. in psychology and often appears on radio and TV in the U.S., Canada, and Great Britain and frequently addresses futurist and libertarian gatherings.

Printed in the USA
CPSIA information can be obtained
at www.ICGtesting.com
JSHW082209140824
68134JS00014B/524